TAKE ME BACK
The Diary of a Machine-gunner in Macedonia, 1916-1919

TAKE ME BACK TO BLIGHTY

The Diary of a Machine-gunner
in Macedonia, 1916-1919

By
George William Burford

Edited by
Alan Wakefield

Introduced and Illustrated by
Susan French Overstreet

To Ruth

Dedicated to the generation that fought the Great War and in particular the men and women of the British Salonika Force whose stories will never be told.

Reveille Press is an imprint of
Tommies Guides Military Booksellers & Publishers

Gemini House
136–140 Old Shoreham Road
Brighton
BN3 7BD

www.tommiesguides.co.uk

First published in Great Britain by
Reveille Press 2016

For more information please visit
www.reveillepress.com

© 2016 Susan French Overstreet

A catalogue record for this book is available
from the British Library

All rights reserved. Apart from any use under UK copyright
law no part of this publication may be reproduced, stored in a retrieval
system, or transmitted, in any form or by any means, without prior written permission of the publisher, nor be
otherwise circulated in any form of binding or cover other than
that in which it is published and without a similar condition being
imposed on the subsequent publisher.

ISBN 978-1-908336-48-4

Cover design by Reveille Press

Printed and bound in Great Britain

Contents

List of Illustrations, Photographs & Maps 10

Acknowledgements 13

Introduction 15

Historical Significance of the Diary 19

Editorial Notes 21

Diary during my Period in Salonika 23

Epilogue 143

List of Illustrations, Photographs & Maps

ILLUSTRATIONS
1. "Inspection by the old man. Got pulled over the coals owing to a bit of mud I had on my clothes," 19 November 1916.
2. "A Taube paid us a visit. Fired about 1000 rounds at him. No luck, so turned my attention to a golden eagle," 14 February 1917
3. "Up rolled the infantry and filled the trenches until we could hardly move," 28 February 1917
4. "Oh, you lovely moon, you have given me away," 30 March 1917
5. "I had just got the range finder in position…when smack a bullet hit the earth in front of my finder and a rifle grenade burst in the trench," 4 April 1917
6. "I expect the old mule thought he had better be moving; he had heard that noise before, so he ran," 10 April 1917
7. "My gun is a lucky gun… Our artillery had opened a gap in the enemy wire and our job was to keep firing…to prevent the Bulgars filling the gap with new wire. Fired 7000 rounds and got shelled twice in the bargain, 20 April 1917
8. "Poor old Georgie, the agony on his face…Well, I'll go back to Blighty. But he will never see Blighty again," 26 April 1917
9. "It was raining lovely and the steam at the bottom was a bit of a torrent," 27 April 1917
10. "Went in for a little boxing. Three hours of it under Corporal Freeman," 28 July 1917
11. "In a skit, I have to be a cowboy, all complete from hat to spurs," 24 December 1917
12. "He was sending over gas, so we made a dash back for our helmets," 6 January 1918
13. "I could hardly find the wire…Up hill, down vale and through bushes on a very dark night, to find a break," 8 August 1918

LIST OF ILLUSTRATIONS, PHOTOGRAPHS & MAPS

14. "Up came the lorries, in went our kits and up we all jumped. At 1:30 p.m. full speed up to the line…we bluffed Johnny that there were more of us than were really coming by sending more lorries forward than were needed to carry us and our kit," 18 September 1918
15. "While on the march to Lake Langasar, my leg cracked up and the commanding officer gave me his horse to ride," 14 October 1918
16. "Goodbye Salonika! Hurray for Blighty!" 1 January 1919
17. "Got orders to go digging at Bowl's Barrow to make emplacement. Worked 'til about 11:00 p.m.," 28 October 1918

PHOTOGRAPHS

1. George Burford shortly after enlisting in the 3/2nd (City of London) Battalion, Royal Fusiliers, March 1915.
2. British dugouts in Happy Valley, a typical camp in a ravine up country in Macedonia, 1916.
3. Remains of the Devil's Eye observation post on the summit of Grand Couronné at Doiran.
4. Men of the 7th South Wales Borderers enjoying a swim during the summer of 1917. (IWM HU 88193)
5. Panorama across the Doiran battlefield in 1918 with Pip Ridge and Grand Couronné on the skyline. Doiran town is on the far side of Lake Doiran.
6. Bulgarian dugouts on the reverse slope of Grand Couronné, 1918. (IWM HU 89730)
7. View across the Doiran battlefield today with Petit Couronné in the centre and Pip Ridge and Grand Couronné in the background.
8. Doiran British Cemetery with the Memorial to the Missing on the hilltop behind.
9. The 10th (Irish) Division Memorial near Rabrovo in FYROM.
10. The BE 12 aircraft in which Lieutenant Paul Denys Montague was shot down and killed on 29 October 1917.
11. The restored 22nd Division Memorial behind Grand Couronné at Doiran.
12. George and Ruth on a picnic.
13. George and Ruth during the 1930s.
14. Ruth Burford with her daughters Ruth, Judy and the twins Jill and Jean, ca.1950.
15. George during the 1940s.

MAPS
1. British area of operations on the Salonika Front.
2. Section of the 1:20,000 British trench map sheet for Smol showing Bulgarian and German positions around 'The Nose.'
3. Bulgarian defences at Doiran 1917 – 1918.
4. The Doiran and Vardar sectors of the front 1916 – 1918.
5. 1:10,000 British trench map sheet Couronné marked up to show the frontage attacked by 22nd Division during the Second Battle of Doiran on 18 September 1918.

Acknowledgements

I WOULD LIKE TO acknowledge the help and expertise of Alan Wakefield, Chairman of the Salonika Campaign Society, who edited the diary in order to place it in historical perspective. He co-authored *Under the Devil's Eye*, the only recent account of British involvement in the Salonika Campaign and his knowledge of this theatre of war is unparalleled. Joining the Salonika Campaign Society tour of the Macedonian battlefields, led by Alan in 2012 enriched my knowledge of my grandfather's experience and began this project of publication. Without his dedication to preserving the memory of the Salonika Campaign, this book would not have been realised and I am very grateful for his kindness, dedication and friendship.

I would also like to acknowledge other members of the Salonika Campaign Society who joined me on the tour for each one of them held their own unique knowledge and perspective and took such an interest in the diary: Keith and Lyn Edmonds, Keith Roberts, Elizabeth Manterfield, Clive Gilbert, Kate and Martin Wills, Andrew Simpson, Seamus Greene, Sean Connolly, Peter Saunders and Jonathan Saunders, as well as the local guides, Romeo Drobarov, Bjuinamin Ibraimov – 'Binko', Gele Stojanovski, Apostolos Nalmbantis and Adrian Wright. Particularly, I would like to thank Jonathan Saunders, for providing extensive comments on the diary; Keith Roberts, who researched individuals named in the diary at the National Archives; and Kate Wills for encouraging me to illustrate the diary. In addition, I would like to thank Robert Alexander and Richard Fisher for their detailed knowledge of the Machine Gun Corps.

Finally, I would like to thank my family and friends who have taken an interest in this project, particularly my mother for answering so many questions about her father; my sisters, Jan and Robin, for helping transcribe and proofread the text; and my dear friend and neighbor Maryanne Lockyer for encouraging me every step of the way to finish this project.

Introduction

WHEN READING MY grandfather's diary, it is easy to get caught up in the excitement of war, with the descriptions of battle and his ability to escape death on a daily basis. However, when recognizing the senseless loss of life, it is horrifying. It is in this contradiction, the human tendency to glorify war and the desire to end it, that makes the diary both a good read and a great lesson.

Historically, this diary is a contribution as a rare primary document: a First World War machine gunner's eyewitness account of frontline mountainous trench warfare. On a personal level, it is the legacy of a grandfather I never knew in life, as he died a decade before I was born. Reading the diary he left behind, I have a sense of my grandfather's experiences, personality, and character. It motivates me to find out more about him, his generation, and the Great War. The diary is particularly significant on the centenary of the war and public awareness focuses on the importance of the war in shaping the world today. As a former educator, it is apparent to me how the diary is a window to the Great War for students of all ages and I am delighted to present it at this time.

During the deluge of heavy rains that pummeled Rhode Island in the spring of 2010, my mother, Ruth Burford French, salvaged her father's First World War diary from her flooded basement. I read the diary for the first time in October of that year and realised the significance of the work not only for my own family history but also for its broader historical value. A transcription of the diary for family members and their descendants became a research project with the goal of publication. While I was transcribing the diary, it was discovered that my brother, Stephen, had another diary and other war memorabilia belonging to our grandfather. The two handwritten diaries were close but not identical in content, covering the same time period and both titled "recopies." It appears that the one in my brother's possession may have been written first.[1]

George Burford shortly after enlisting in the 3/2nd (City of London) Battalion, Royal Fusiliers, March 1915.

---

[1] There are a number of reasons that we believe my mother's copy is a later version. First, the first few pages begin in what is believed to be my grandmother's handwriting, and they were not acquainted until after the war. Second, he spells Salonika with a "k" rather than a "c" in the later version. This "k" spelling is the accepted spelling in military history, so possibly he made that correction later. Third, the second copy is clearly edited to soften his opinions of the war effort and his superior officers. Fourth, he includes some explanatory details that are retrospective to educate the reader.

INTRODUCTION

The original diary was written on scraps of paper in the trenches, as noted by George in the diary, and was used to recopy the surviving diaries. The first diary was probably written during George's convalescence in early 1919 and the second about the time George and Ruth first met in the early 1920s, although we only know for certain it was written before his death on January 9, 1946. Despite our many theories, we cannot be certain why George Burford chose to include material in one diary, while omitting it from the other. This is one of the many reasons that both diaries are so intriguing.

The decision was taken to use the first diary as the basis for this published text and to incorporate the 'new' elements from the second copy into the main text or as footnotes. The diary is a rare and vivid snapshot that captures an important turning point in history and an eyewitness account of one of the most gruesome wars in history. On an individual level, it is the adventure of a young London boy in a far-off land. Well-versed in the stories of Rudyard Kipling, George Burford was drawn into the war fervor that engulfed the British Empire in the early twentieth century. George enlisted in the Territorial Force on March 2, 1915 with the 3/2nd (City of London) Battalion, Royal Fusiliers. He later joined the Machine Gun Corps, possibly indicating that he had already specialized as a machine gunner. Like many young men attempting to join the colours in England at that time he gave, or was given, an older age upon enlisting. George was seventeen at the time of his enlistment and, by law, was not able to serve overseas until the age of nineteen. However, he went overseas in October 1916, travelling to France en-route to deployment in Macedonia.

George was in Salonika for two years and exposed to all aspects of trench warfare: the ever present chance of death, including that of close companions; disease; poison gas; shellshock and life-threatening wounds. He was trained and skilled in numerous military specialisms as machine-gunner, rangefinder and signaller. His coverage of the war from the perspective of a frontline soldier in the mountainous Salonika theatre is unprecedented to my knowledge. Indeed, the fact that a machine gunner on the front line had the forethought and discipline to keep a diary is remarkable. His careful recopy of his battered diary is testimony to the importance he placed upon his experience.

Despite his modest background, George's keen observation of his circumstances displays an intelligence and character that transcends class. He offers an astute, honest and often humorous description of people and events. Further, it may be his London streetwiseness that kept him alive! George was born in Lambeth, the son of a potter, Herbert Henry Burford and his wife, Elizabeth Selina Jones. Lambeth was, and still is, a working class neighborhood across the Thames from Parliament, though the waterfront is now lined with modern office buildings, modest terraced houses lie beyond. I have wandered through the neighborhood on my way to visit the Imperial War Museum, wondering about both of my grandparents and their young life before and after the war. My grandmother lived in Southwark within walking distance along the Thames. Her father, Robert Castor Shelston, owned a butchers shop and proudly displayed the sign "by appointment of Her Majesty, the Queen." The marriage of my grandparents was not as likely before the war given the rigid class stratifications of Edwardian Britain. However, after the war, with so many young men killed, it was a different world, both socially and economically. In fact, the post-war economy led to my grandparent's emigration to the United States in search of better prospects.

Historical Significance of the Diary

◦∼◦

O NLY A FEW published accounts of machine gunners' experiences in World War I exist: a compilation by C.E. Crutchley, *Machine Gunner, 1914-1918*; George Coppard's autobiography, *With a Gun in Cambrai*; and *Mud, Blood and Bullets* by Edward Rowbotham, each written some time after the war's end. Equally rare are detailed histories dealing specifically with the Salonika Front: *Military Operations Macedonia,* the two volume official history compiled by Cyril Falls in 1933 and 1935, *The Gardeners of Salonika* by Alan Palmer, and Alan Wakefield and Simon Moody's *Under the Devil's Eye: Britain's Forgotten Army at Salonika, 1915-1918*. A recent publication, *Balkan Breakthrough: The Battle of Dobro Pole 1918* by Richard C. Hall, describes events from the Bulgarian perspective.

The histories recognize the importance of the two Battles of Doiran as crucial supporting operations to major Allied offensives in the Balkans. In both battles the British XII Corps managed to achieve its strategic objective of pinning down Bulgarian units at Doiran to prevent them moving west of the River Vardar to contest the main Franco-Serbian offensive. During the first battle (April - May 1917) the British effort was to no avail as the main Allied advance was quickly halted by the Bulgarians. However, during the second battle (18 – 19 September 1918) the sacrifices at Doiran assisted the Allies maintain their momentum after French and Serbian forces had forced a passage through Bulgarian mountain-top positions in the Battle of Dobrepolje, which determined Allied victory on the Salonika Front.[2] George Burford was in the center of both battles.

---

[2] The First World War would eventually involve thirty-two nations, but the major powers fighting on the Salonika Front were, on the Allied/Entente side:

In the first, he fills the dangerous jobs of rangefinder and machine gunner in preparation for and during the battle. He describes the deaths around him, including two of his "pals:" George McWilliam and Fred Farthing, both during the First Battle of Doiran in 1917. Later, after being wounded in the leg by shrapnel on 6 January 1918, George works his way back from hospital to the front lines by serving as signaler. In September 1918, George is again in the thick of the battle, but as signaler he is able to give a wider account of the action. During the Second Battle of Doiran, British and Greek forces manage to secure Petit Couronné, the main bastion of the Bulgarian frontline but they again fail to push the 9th (Pleven) Division from Pip Ridge and Grand Couronné. However, despite this apparent defeat, George stands at the Devil's Eye observation post on the summit of Grand Couronné within days after the battle, looking out at the carnage. He states simply: "war, it's a rotten game."

For the British especially, the Salonika Front was viewed as a drain on military resources that could better be used on the Western Front. Due to lack of tangible results in the campaign until late 1918, there was a tendency for many contemporary opinion formers to disparage and denigrate service on the Salonika front, something of which George Burford and his comrades in the British Salonika Force were well aware.[3] But, as documented by Wakefield and Moody, the men and women of the British Salonika Front dealt with difficult mountainous terrain for which they were ill prepared, they continually faced widespread disease, and they fought an enemy on its own turf that was war-hardened by the two Balkan Wars. The British Salonika Force was indeed forgotten, as they served far from home and had limited opportunity to enjoy home leave to Britain during their service.[4]

Britain, France, Greece, Italy, Russia and Serbia and for the Central Powers Bulgaria, supported by German, Austro-Hungarian and Turkish contingents.

[3] See entry on 18 September 1918.

[4] Wakefield and Moody describe the unique conditions of the British Salonika Front.

Editorial Notes

APART FROM AMALGAMATING entries from the two diaries, editing of the text has been limited primarily to correction of spelling and grammar plus improvements to punctuation to ensure ease of reading. Abbreviations are spelled out for clarification, for example: *brigade* for *br.*, *division* for *div.*, *company* for *coy*. Similarly, dates are written out in full. When the author engages in a conversation, quotations are inserted to make the dialogue more understandable. If a word is indecipherable, {?} is inserted in its place. Additionally, place and personal names have been standardized, the former to correspond with the spelling given in the two volumes of the British Official History of the campaign.

In the text George Burford uses the standard nicknames "Tommy" for British troops, "Johnny" for the Bulgarians and "the Hun", "Fritz" and "Jerry," for the Germans. Of the three latter terms, "Jerry" is much better known from the Second World War. However, it was coined during the earlier conflict, coming either from an alteration of "German" or following the introduction of the distinctive German steel helmet (stalhelm), which was through to look like a chamber pot, already commonly known as a "Jerry".

Footnotes are included to define unfamiliar words and to highlight events, places or people of historical significance. The War Diary of the 66th Machine Gun Company from The National Archives proved an invaluable source for supporting the events described in the diary. A copy of the diary was sent to me in digital format by Alan Wakefield in November of 2011. It comprises 110 pages covering the period from July 1916 until the disbanding of the unit in March 1919. A war diary is a handwritten account compiled by an officer (sometimes the C.O.) of a unit or formation and then signed-off each month by the C.O. as an accurate record of that unit's or formation's war service. Copies of war diaries were submitted at regular intervals to GHQ and eventually were filed with the War Office to help with the writing up of campaign official histories and regimental or corps histories. Where entries in the 66th MGC war diary correspond to activity in my grandfather's diary, giving interesting insights from the unit's perspective, these have been incorporated as footnotes to the text.

Diary during my Period in Salonika

Re-copy of Diary taken whilst in Active Service Leaving France for Salonika, October 26, 1916

29 October 1916
Entrained and left Le Havre, arrived Versailles 12:00 a.m., arrived Tuvisy 12:00 p.m. on the 30th, arrived Orange, 6:00 p.m. on the 30th, left Orange 10:00 p.m. Passed through Lyons and arrived Avignon at 12:00 a.m., on the 31st. Arrived Marseilles 8:00 p.m. on the 1st of November. Embarked for Salonika and sailed on the Transylvania[5] at 1:00 a.m., 2nd November, arrived at Salonika on 5th of November, and landed on the 6th.

6 November 1916
Landed at Salonika, saw Taube[6] shelled and marched from the harbour through the streets of Salonika to Summer Hill Camp. Many locals about, all distinguishable by their national dress. The sun was beating down on us at about 90 in the shade and the dust on the roads was being kicked up in clouds as we marched, it was not very comfortable, but we get over these things and were thankful when we reached camp.

---

[5] The *Transylvania* was a Cunard passenger liner commissioned as a troopship in May of 1915. She was travelling between Marseilles and Alexandria when torpedoed and sunk by German U-boat U63 off Cape Vado, near Savona in the Gulf of Genoa on May 4, 1917. Despite two escorting Japanese destroyers being on hand to rescue survivors, 10 crew members, 29 officers and 373 soldiers lost their lives.

[6] Generic name given by British soldiers to German aircraft during the First World War. The term dates from 1914 when the Germans used a number of monoplanes with distinctive swept-back, bird-like wings. This type of aircraft was the Taube (German for Dove). The name entered the vocabulary of British soldiers and was used to describe any enemy aircraft.

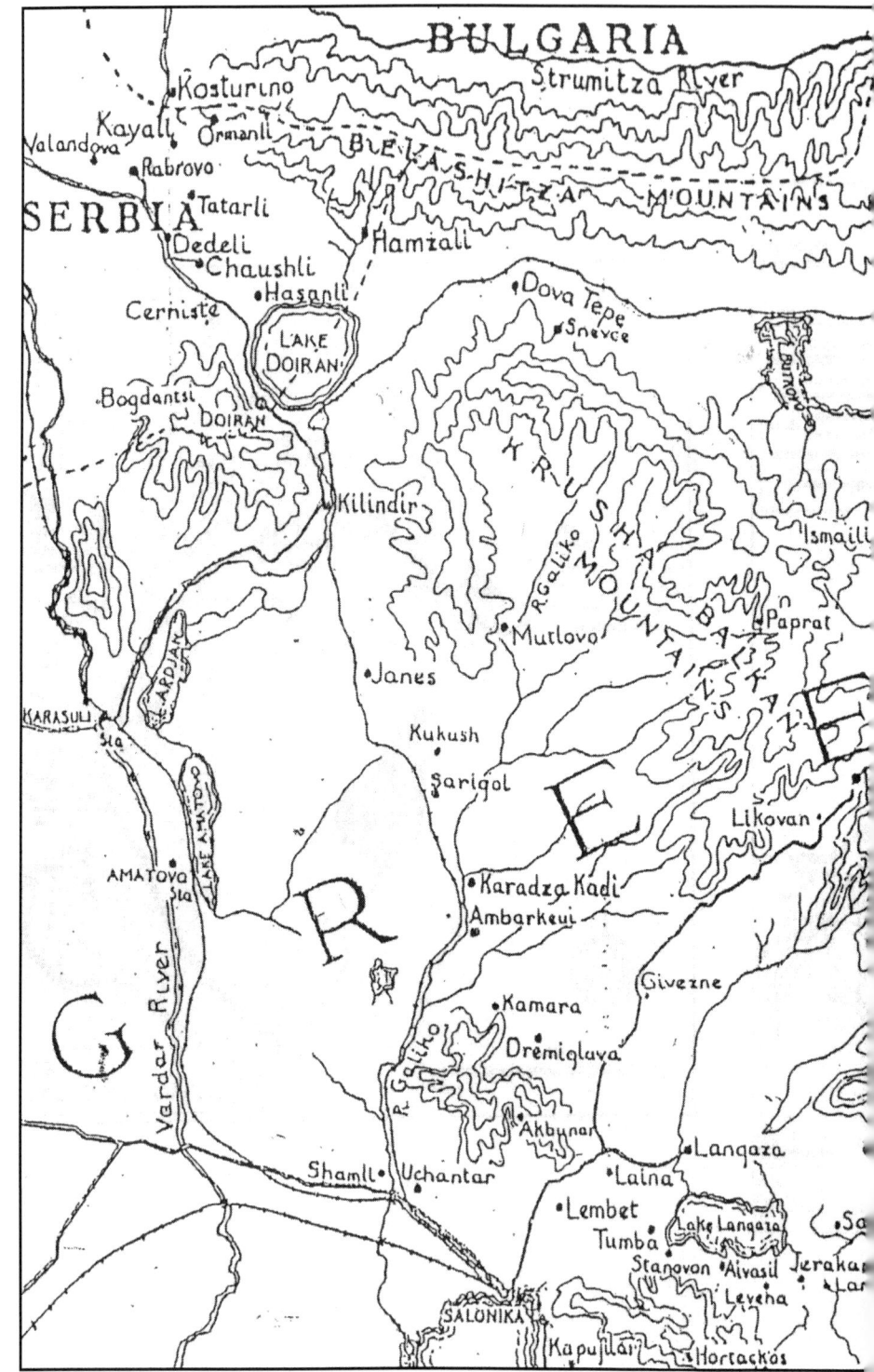

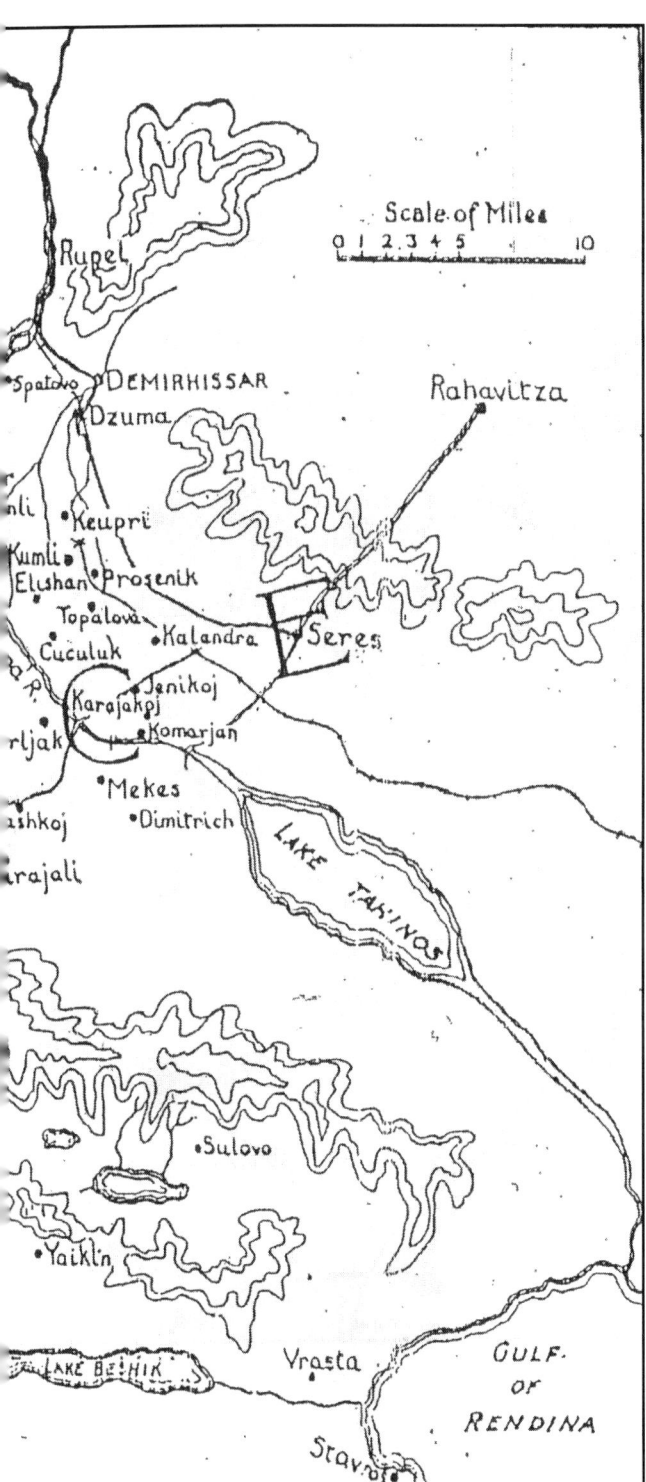

British area of operations on the Salonika Front.

7 November 1916
Paraded for winter clothing, what the Dickens for? I cannot understand when it is hotter than a mid-summer day in England, but I suppose the army knows best.

8 November 1916
Detailed out in companies. Put in the 66th Brigade with Charlie Muncey and Fred Farthing.[7]

9 November 1916
Attached to the 22nd Division[8].

10 November 1916
Inspection by about ten different officers and messed about in general all day.

11 November 1916
Same old process as yesterday. Rumor that we are off up the line tomorrow.

12 November 1916
Yes, the rumor was right. At 10:00 a.m. this morning we started. After marching for about four hours, which seemed like twenty-four,

---

[7] George was assigned to the 66th Company, Machine Gun Company within 22nd Division when he arrived in Salonika in November of 1916. The 66th Company, MGC had left Grantham on 4 July 1916 and embarked for Salonika the following day from Keyham Dockyard onboard HMT Minnetonka. The Company arrived at Salonika on 13 July.

[8] The 22nd Division was established in September 1914 as part of Army Order 388 authorizing Kitchener's Third New Army. The Division left Flesselles, France in September 1915, and moved by train to Marseilles to begin embarking for Salonika in October and November. The Division was assigned to XII Corps of the British Salonika Force and served on the Doiran Sector longer than any other British formation. The 22nd Division was disbanded by March 13, 1919. During its period of active service, 22nd Division suffered 7,728 casualties with larger numbers sick with malaria, dysentery and other diseases.

we arrived at Dudular Station and entrained, or rather entrucked I ought to say. After picking out the softest spot, I thought the best thing would be to try and get a sleep. After about two hours, I woke up stiff and cramped, and to my dismay, I discovered that we had traveled only fifteen miles. We had sixty to go, so goodness knows how long it would take. (If I remember rightly, the engine that pulled us was from England and belonged to the South Eastern and Chatham Railway, so that accounted for it I suppose). At 4 p.m. we arrived at Kilindir and were glad to detrain. But the journey was not ended. Kilindir was situated on a plain and facing the town at a distance was a range of hills and over the hilltops we could see the flash of the guns, so we knew we were not far from the line. At the foot of the hills dotted here and there were British camps. On our left was a great lake by the name of Ardzan. On our right was the plain. After the spell of about one hour, we proceeded on to our destination and arrived at Karasouli which was at the foot of the hills and for the present were attached to our company transport before proceeding to the company tomorrow. Jove! Hasn't it become suddenly cold? And it is now raining and coming through our bivvy.[9] I'm getting wet, so I think I shall pack up. If the bivvy does not blow down, I shall be surprised.

13 November 1916
It is 7:00 a.m. and we are going to get breakfast. What a rotten night we have had, soaking wet and bivvy blown down about half a dozen times. We all got soaking wet. A very enjoyable night! At 4:00 p.m. this afternoon we had to pack up to join the company up the line. We arrived at Ardzan Ravine at about 8:00 p.m. Mud everywhere and a drizzling rain and very much fed up. Upon reaching the company, we were put in separate sections[10]. Charlie, Fred and myself were

---

[9] "Bivvy" is slang for bivouac, a simple tent made from two waterproof sheets. Each British soldier carried one waterproof sheet and a tent-pole, allowing every two men to construct a bivvy for temporary accommodation.

[10] The strength of a Machine Gun Company varied during the war, but was usually around 144-150 men. Each Company took its number from the Infantry Brigade to which it was attached. It comprised 4 Sections of 4 Vickers guns (16 guns in total), with each Section usually consisting of 2 Subalterns, 2 Sergeants,

to go right away up in the trenches to join No.1 section. A chap was waiting to take us and off we went, up one hill, now another, through stream and mud and whizz-bangs.[11] *Then a voice in front by our escorts "Damn, I'm lost." Great news! How long we walked and where I do not know. At last we saw a light shining through the opening of a dugout. After being put on the right road, we arrived at the communication trenches, and reached the Section, reported to the officer in command, and were sent to a dugout. What a rotten place, water, water, everywhere. We cleared what water we could back into the trench and got down to it, to the best of our possibility.*

14 November 1916
After a most uncomfortable night trying to keep clear of the water that filled the dugout, we were called for breakfast at 7:30 a.m. The boys were just standing down. Saw the officer after breakfast and I was put on No.1 gun with Charlie. Fred was attached to No.2 gun. Feeling rather tired we went back to the dugout and bailed out the water and laid out our waterproof sheets and went to sleep until dinnertime. After dinner we thought that we would like a look round, but as there was not much to see, we altered our minds and thought we would leave it until another time. At 6:00 p.m. we stood to and that gave us the opportunity to see all we wanted to. On our left were the French and Serbs, we almost joining the French. In front, a bit of narrow plain, then a hill called "The Nose."[12] *Beyond the ravines and hills, in front of The Nose, Jerry and the Bulgar trenches. I am on sentry with Charlie Muncey at 9:00 p.m., so I shall now finish for tonight.*

---

2 Corporals, 16 Privates, 5 Drivers (for horse-drawn transport wagons) and 2 Batmen. To this total of 116 must be added HQ staff such as the C.O. (a Major or Captain), a Subaltern, Company Sergeant Major, Company Quartermaster Sergeant and Transport Sergeant, as well as other support staff such as an Artificer, Shoeing-Smith, Saddler, 4 Signallers, 8 Range-takers, 8 Scouts, 3 Drivers, 1 Storeman, 2 Cooks, 2 Batmen and 2 RAMC Privates.

[11] Slang term used by British solders for shells fired by enemy field guns.

[12] 'The Nose' was the name given to a prominent hill just to the north-east of Macukovo village. On 'The Nose' was sited an entrenched strongpoint, which formed part of the main Bulgarian – German position just east of the River Vardar.

DIARY DURING MY PERIOD IN SALONIKA

15 November 1916
At 9:00 p.m. last night, Charlie and I done our first turn at sentry on the Salonika Front. It was rather quiet except for a terrific bombardment between the French and Bulgar. All we had was just one or two over, which made us duck a bit owing to being unable to tell the flight of the shells. In time you can tell pretty near whereabouts they are going to fall. But today nothing really exciting happened, just kept to the dugout all day.

16 November 1916
Done our usual sentry last night. It is done in pairs with one man looking out while the other sleeps in a cut in the trench. The cut is about six feet long and two feet wide and about six inches up from the bottom of the trench. If the sentry thinks something is likely to happen he kicks the fellow in the cut – the nearest part that is handy – and I can assure you some of them don't kick lightly, sometimes like a mule! The rest of the gun teams sleep in shell-proof dugouts but it's a pity they are not waterproof. So, of course, on sentry I was alone with my own thoughts and they were not worth writing about. All today we just packed up ready to be relieved by No.4 Section. They came at 8:00 p.m., took over position and we moved back in the Ardzan Ravine, unpacked the kit off mules and got down to it.

17 November 1916
Done nothing today. Just had our meals and slept.

18 November 1916
Tidied up in general and cleaned ourselves of mud for general inspection tomorrow. Hear that after attacking for four days the French and Serbs have taken Monastir[13].

---

[13] The liberation of Monastir was the culmination of an Allied offensive in Macedonia launched on 12 September 1916. The victory came just before the winter snows forced the closing down of the offensive. Although the town remained under shellfire its capture was a great morale boost for the Allies as Monastir was the first major town in Serbia to be liberated from the Bulgarians.

Section of the 1:20,000 British trench map sheet for Smol showing Bulgarian and German positions around 'The Nose.'

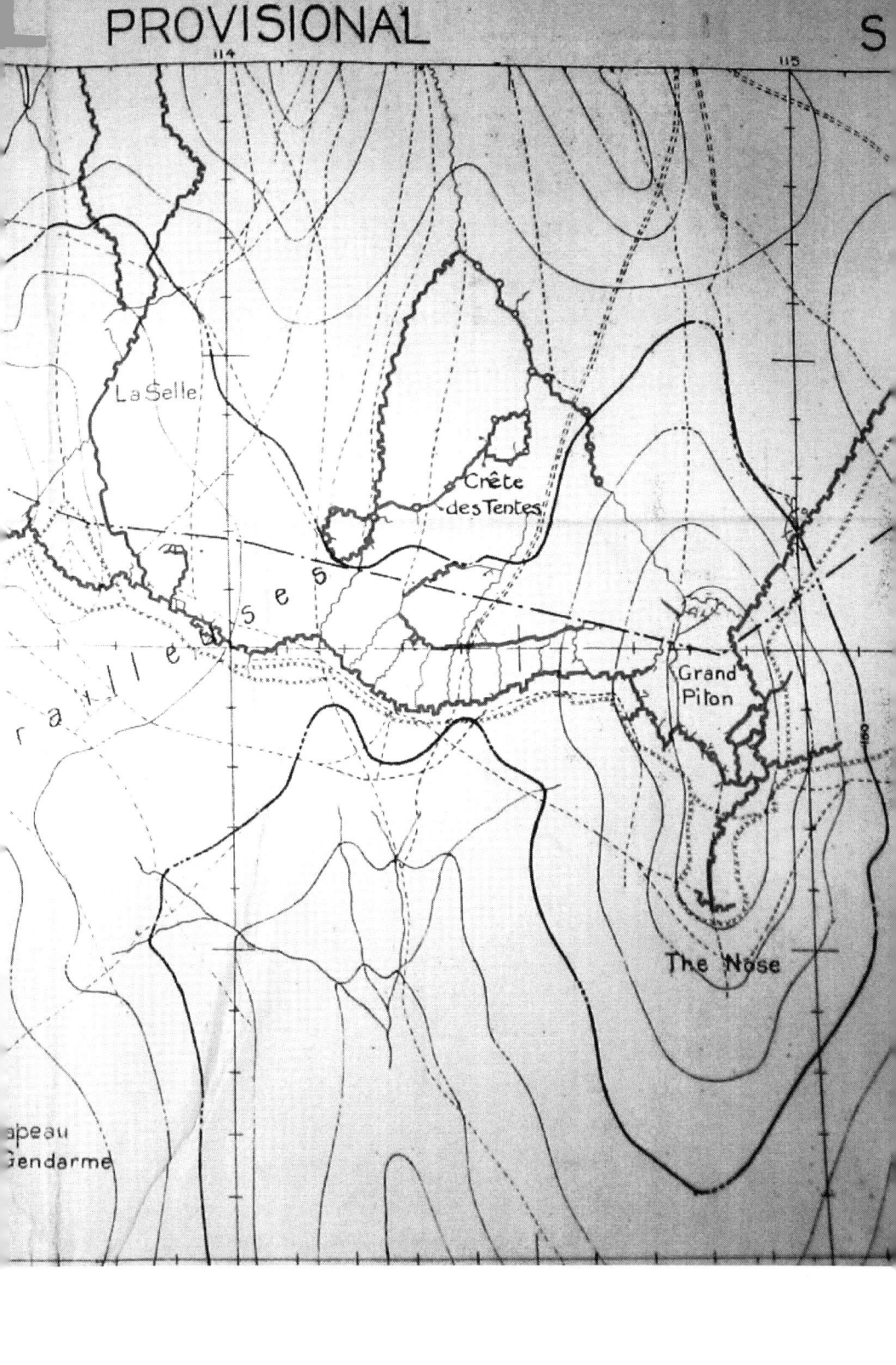

"Inspection by the old man. Got pulled over the coals owing to a bit of mud I had on my clothes," 19 November 1916.

19 November 1916
Inspection by the old man. Got pulled over the coals owing to a little mud I had on my clothes. Tomorrow we go in the trenches again, but during the rest we have been digging dugouts and emplacements and being shelled everyday. But nothing really important happened.

DIARY DURING MY PERIOD IN SALONIKA

18 December 1916[14]
After writing my diary for the last month on scraps of paper I lost it! But, I will try to sum it up. Firstly it has been raining nearly all the time causing small streams to become raging torrents, dugout to fall in and twice we had to dig fellows out. Two men were partly buried, their faces and feet showing only and the rain pelted at them, making them look perfect pictures. Rations and cigs have been short which was the worst thing that could have happened. Charlie and I took extra care of a cigarette we had between us and all we could do was one draw at a time and wrap it up in paper and save it for another time. Fred had no baccy at all so he tried dried tea leaves in his pipe. Now that is all right if you are about five miles away from the smoker but get in a small dugout- it's awful. Anyway, Charlie and I thought it was best for us to get out in the rain. Still, Fred enjoyed his smoke, so what did it matter. In the end Charlie and I came down to cigarette

---

14 66th MGC War Diary, 1-9 December 1916: No operations on our immediate front of note took place. The infantry sent on frequent patrols but seldom encountered the enemy. A great deal of labor was put into the construction of an alternative line of defense from WAGON HILL to A4 and a reserve or 2nd line defense from A1 to BAJALCA. The weather conditions were very bad indeed. A large number of dugouts collapsed. The health of the company was good not withstanding the weather. Orders were given by the Brigade HQ that the company was to be kept up to strength by battalion detaching men to replace casualties.
10-31 December 1916: No operations of note took place during this period. The line from WAGON HILL to A4 (now K4) was nearly completed and the tactical wire on the A1-BAJALCA line was marked out. Reconnaissance of rewired lines and neighboring were carried out. Sections in support and reserve were given a large amount of discipline drill as the continuous holding of trenches without any operations taking place was beginning to have a bad effect on the men. Great difficulty was experienced in obtaining boots, clothing, etc. from ordnance. The health of the company was very good, several men returning from hospital and very few going. There were no cases of trench feet. A raid on enemy trenches NE of the NOSE was arranged but had to be abandoned at the last moment owing to the latest aeroplane photographs showing works and wire previously unknown to us. 1 section of the Coy were to have been employed in the raid. An enemy aeroplane was forced down by the machine gun fire of No. 1 section under 2nd Lieut. Hamilton.

ends and brown paper. We did guard in turn and had nothing to think of except how cushy we should be if there had not been a war on.

We were shelled almost every day and that meant either ducking in mud or diving in dugouts if they happened to be handy, but otherwise nothing really important happened.

Today, we moved up the line at 7:30 p.m. I had to lead a gun mule and what a brute it was[15]. (But of course all mules are.) Instead of me leading the blighter, it led me and well I knew it. He pulled me through bushes until I was scratched all over, until we reached a shallow ravine or ditch. It had been raining all day and the mud was nice and slippery. We had no bridge to cross, but had to go down the slope, cross a stream about two feet deep and up the other side. The width of the stream was not wide, easy to step over, but my luck was out. Just as I got to the edge to come down to cross, the officer on the other side shone his confounded torch light. Up shot my mules head, jerking me off my feet and down the slope. I slid into the confounded water, while a voice above asked me if I was alright. Drenched to the skin I clambered up and after catching the mule I wreaked my vengeance on him and relieved myself by swearing and cursing him. I got the mule across the ditch and further along the road where we

---

[15] In July 1916 the War Office approved a pack transport scale devised by Generals Mahon and Milne to make the BSF mobile in Macedonia where there existed few roads suitable for wheeled vehicles. Machine gun companies were amongst the units entirely given over to pack mule transport. In total a company was allotted 102 mules with 61 drivers, plus a further 14 mules and 7 drivers for the supply and baggage train. Within this establishment each MG section had 4 mules (with 4 drivers) each to carry one Vickers gun, tripod and spare parts; 8 mules (with 4 drivers) to carry 1st ammunition supply of 3,500 rounds (in belts) per gun; 10 mules (with 5 drivers) carrying 2nd ammunition supply of 18,000 rounds (in boxes) per section, plus signals equipment and sandbags. From spring 1917, machine gun companies began returning to wheeled vehicle transport exchanging mules for 18 wagons, 43 horses and 22 drivers, plus 1 wagon with 2 heavy draught horses and a driver for the supplies and baggage. Within this transport scale a MG section was allotted 2 wagons (with 8 draught horse and 4 drivers) for guns, tripods, spares and ammunition and an additional wagon (with 2 draught horses and 1 driver) for the 2nd ammunition supply.

unpacked and took our positions from the 67th Machine Gun Company. I was feeling great and cursing everybody, especially the Hun. And so I remained all night and eventually got dry. Rather a long job.

19 December 1916
A rather quiet day.

20 December 1916
Things liven up a bit.

21 December 1916
Something doing. Our boys sending over everything. Kept it up all day.

22 December 1916
Guns still going strong.

23 December 1916
Cheshires made an attack on The Nose at 8:30 p.m.[16] and we had quite a lively time of it all night (don't bullets sound like bees) but luckily there were not many casualties. Things quietened down by morning.

24 December 1916
Went to headquarters to bring up new draft just out from England and to get canteen stuff for Christmas. Got that ready and put into sacks and back to the line with goods and the new boys towing behind. They were bombarding us with questions but we could only tell them to wait and see. They will soon get used to it. Got back to the trenches with men, took them to Lieutenant Hamilton ('Ham')[17] and dumped the Xmas stuff in his dug-out.

---

[16] This diary entry refers to a feint attack involving the 12th Cheshires, with much supporting artillery fire, to give the Bulgarians the impression that an attack was intended. This appears to have been successful given the fact that even George believed a raid had gone in at The Nose.

[17] Lieutenant Lowther Lee Hamilton, born 9 March 1894, a former bank clerk from Cumberland. Hamilton joined the Westmorland and Cumberland Yeomanry as a private at Cockermouth on 9 November 1914. He applied

25 December 1916
Today was very quiet but then it was Christmas Day. Our boys did not fire a gun and neither did Jerry. After standing down in the evening, all the men that could be spared went to the officers' dugout and had a little sing-song. Also, rum and to make it a little more Christmassy, nuts and oranges but unfortunately, no turkey or pudding. Still we enjoyed ourselves under the circumstances and for a while forgot the war.[18]

26 December 1916
Rather cold, could hardly load the gun, so the officer gave me a double issue of rum and it took effect on me and made me tell everyone that I was drunk. My gun position is at a point a little further forward than

---

for a commission on 15 March 1915 and was sent as a 2nd Lieutenant to the 6th Border Regiment. On 12 February, Hamilton transferred to the Machine Gun Corps. He travelled out to Salonika with the 66th Machine Gun Company. Between 16 September and 3 December 1916, Hamilton was away from his unit suffering from malaria and septic sores, the latter ailment getting him a few weeks in RAMC establishments on Malta. Just under three weeks after returning to 66th MG Company, Hamilton was promoted to temporary lieutenant. On 26 February 1917, Hamilton was tried by a General Court Martial for being drunk on duty. Entering a plea of Not Guilty, Hamilton was found Guilty and received a severe reprimand. The date of his promotion to lieutenant was also moved to the date the court martial concluded. Hamilton spent most of July 1917 at No.4 Canadian General Hospital suffering from dysentery. On 4 November 1917, Hamilton was admitted to 31 CCS and then 21st Stationery Hospital with a bullet wound to his left forearm. He rejoined his unit once more on 19 December 1917. Another spell in hospital followed at the end of June 1918, lasting until just before Hamilton left for leave to the UK on 26 July. This period of leave kept Hamilton out of the Second Battle of Doiran. He returned to Salonika on 5 November 1918 and rejoined 66th MG Company three weeks later. On 5 February 1919, Hamilton was made an acting captain whilst serving as second in command of 66th MG Company. On 9 April, Hamilton was posted to 81st MG Company and embarked for Batoum in Georgia. He began his journey back to the UK from Constantinople on 30 August and was formally demobilized with effect from 12 September 1919.

[18] For troops in the First World War, Christmas often witnessed a slackening off in the intensity of fighting. Soldiers in the Salonika Campaign were lucky enough to enjoy two Christmases each year as the Bulgarians, being Orthodox, then celebrated the day on 7 January, rather than 25 December.

the front line. During the day we put the gun in the small dugout with the nozzle pointing through a small hole so that the gun is hidden from Jerry while its light, and should Jerry attack by day we can fire at him from under cover. During the night we take the gun out and place it in a small 'V' shaped cutting in the parapet with the gun just above the top of the trench.

27 December 1916
Went on air picquet[19] but nothing doing, not even a bird to shoot at.

British dugouts in Happy Valley, a typical camp in a ravine up country in Macedonia, 1916.

28 December 1916
Charlie, Rob and myself had to go to HQ to get three boxes of ammunition. Reached Cheshires HQ, which lay in a deep ravine. The dugouts were built on either side and the bottom of the ravine for some distance is under observation from The Nose and one has to cross the ravine at that very point. Just as we were crossing the bottom - Whizz! Old Charlie went on all fours in the mud. I could not move; neither could Rob. We just stuck still and waited for the burst. It did not come. It was a dud and a good thing too. It entered the earth but twenty yards from

---

[19] Machine-gun being used in anti-aircraft role to defend camp.

us. Whew! What a relief. Then we ran and dived into a dugout. Charlie looked a picture, covered in mud all down his front. After about five minutes we started again and had to go over a hill. When we reached the top over came another shell. Then we parted company and all flew in different directions. A beautiful coalbox[20] burst about 200 yards away. I began to think Jerry had seen us. We made for the next ravine as quick as possible and sat down for a little smoke before going on. Thank goodness we have only one more hill to go over, so up we got to get over. Almost over when - look out! – another one is coming - so we tried to race it but as usual it beat us. It was a bit high and flew over the hill and hit the next one. Got to our HQ, received ammunition and returned to trenches in quietness. This is the life!

29 December 1916
Nothing much doing today.

30 December 1916
Still quiet.

31 December 1916
Very quiet today until about midnight. On the stroke of 12 the Royal Artillery opened out on Jerry just for a New Year's greeting and gave them a hot half hour.

11 January 1917[21]
The diary pages I thought I had lost were now discovered at the bottom of my kit bag! All I did today was air picquet, fired at a Taube, but it was a bit too high.

---

[20] Slang term used by British soldiers for a German 5.9-inch shell which produced a cloud of black smoke when exploding.

[21] 66th MGC War Diary, 1-31 January 1917: "No operations of note took place during this period. A great amount of fatigue work both by day and night was put into improving existing emplacements and dugouts and in making new emplacements and dugouts in the "J" line between ARDZAN and WAGON HILL. The vicinity of the Coy HQ was frequently shelled chiefly by 5.9. This was probably due to the erection of large quantities of tactical wire at the reserve lines and the fact that men working on this wire must have been visible on

DIARY DURING MY PERIOD IN SALONIKA

12 January 1917
Johnny's 'New Year's Day. Expected a bit of bombardment at 12:00 p.m. but he did not do it. But evidently our boys thought that they would give it to Johnny instead. At Midnight they let rip and kept it up until 4:00 a.m. in the morning of the 13th. Johnny stuck it until 2:00 p.m., when Fred relieved me off sentry. I tried to sleep in the small emplacement beside the gun, but the crash of the shells that Johnny spat up would not let me and it made me bounce up and down, so sleep was out of the question. I came out and had a look. I believe Johnny anticipated an attack by the flares he wasted and artillery and machine gun ammunition he sent over. Anyway, he did not do us any damage.

13 January 1917
Nothing doing but a few whizz-bangs over.

---

occasion from PT 535. A great improvement was made in the transport for the benefit of both animals and personnel. Machine gun fire opened on several occasions at enemy aircraft that were flying lower than usual. Apparently, there were no anti-aircraft guns in action. Although no aeroplane was brought down, they invariably were driven off when fired at by Vickers Guns at ranges under 1200 feet. Sections were frequently practiced in night alarms and became able to get ready in under 20 minutes (this applies to reserve positions starting with their boots off). I received a visit from XII Corp MGO who went very thoroughly into the administrative side of MG Coy work and asked for suggestions as to improving the establishment of MG Coy. Several suggestions were made: Sections in support and reserve and transport personnel were given range practice with machine guns, rifles and revolvers. Experiments were made in night firing with the luminous sights with very satisfying results. During the month the amount of office work became very great indeed and I was employed at it for 12 hours of the 24. There was a case of an important message being sent by an officer of the company which should not have been sent. A court of inquiry was held, which found that the officer sent the message, though not having been informed of a certain artillery demonstration which was taking place. As the guns in the front line had been tactically placed under the OC Section in whose area they were, I am of opinion, that it was the duty of the OC sector to have informed the officer concerned of all that was going on....The health of the company during this month was very good. Several men returned from hospital and the company kept to strength.

14 January 1917
Things a bit busy.

15 January 1917
More busy.

16 January 1917
A day doing air picquet.

17 January 1917
Went to build dugout for the cook. Got shelled, so laid low until Stand To. When we went to mount the gun for the night, a shell dumped itself on our day emplacement and blew it in. Gun turned round, tangent sight bent, ammunition box thrown under tripod. Pulled the gun out of the mess and cleaned her up a bit. Gun was not damaged so much as first thought, so she was still able to do her bit of work at night when needed.

18 January 1917
Went on air picquet. Poor old Lieutenant Hamilton, he cannot leave us alone. Fussed about us all day until we got fed up with him.

19 January 1917
Relieved and went back for rest at Corsika.[22]

20 January 1917
Slept all day.

21 January 1917
Had to put mud on new tents to disguise them like a chunk of earth[23].

---

[22] Chauchitza or Causica – site of British camps and a station on the Karasouli – Kilindir Branch Railway.

[23] A basic camouflaging technique to break up the outline of tents to make them less conspicuous especially from the air.

DIARY DURING MY PERIOD IN SALONIKA

22 January 1917
Still throwing mud about.

23 January 1917
And still doing it.

24 January 1917
Got orders to pack up equipment. Nos.1 and 2 guns for going up the line again.

25 January 1917
Started building dugouts in a ravine just behind front line but did not do much today. Looked over souvenirs, too much to cart about, so dumped them.

26 January 1917
Still on dugouts. Isn't it beastly cold?

27 January 1917
Expect to be kept on dugouts for some time. I am not going to put "still on dugouts" every day so I'll give the diary a rest.

5 February 1917[24]
We have been at the dugouts until today. It is the 5th of February. We have been getting up stakes and timber and iron quadrants. They are

---

[24] 66th MGC War Diary, 1 - 10 February 1917: There were no operations of note during this period. The health of the company was good notwithstanding the severe weather. The commanding officer was attached to the 13th Manchester Regiment as acting 2nd in command from the 5th. Lieutenant DEAS took over temporary command of the company on the 5th. The transport was inspected by the GOC 66th Brigade and ADVS 22nd Division. Detailed defense .... and alarm orders were drawn up for all sections at Company HQ. Runners received continuous training. The "J" line was given up as a possible front line defense and a new line (BJ) sited. Positions and tactical wire for MG in this latter wire decided on and approved by GOC. New tactical wire positions in I sector were decided on and work on them commenced. A draft of 13

going to be some dugouts, the best we have made so far and will be really shell proof.

6 February 1917
Today we are about half done and while getting out a lump of rock we found a nest of snakes, about fifteen of them, several small ones and large. The longest was five feet long. Then the fun commenced. One snake I had a particular liking for doing a bolt and went to earth. So got a stiff branch and digging it well into the hole, heaved it up. Up shot earth and snake to about twenty feet in the air. As none of us liked the idea of it falling on us, we scattered in all directions. When he landed we started to poke him with sticks. The snake started to get a bit lively hissing at us in turns, so I chopped its head off with a spade, skinned him and preserved the skin. Think I shall keep it.

13 February 1917[25]
We have almost finished the dugouts, putting six to seven feet of rocks and earth on top of the quadrants to help make it shell proof. It has been very cold.

14 February 1917
I was on air picquet all today at an emplacement about 100 yards from our dugout. A Taube paid us a visit. Fired about 1000 rounds at him but no luck, so turned my attention to a golden eagle but was glad afterwards I did not hit it.

---

men arrived from the Machine Gun Training Center. These men had not had sufficient training to take their places in the front line.

[25] 66th MGC War Diary, 11 – 20 February: "No operations of note took place during this period. Enemy aircraft became more active and were over our lines frequently. They occasionally dropped bombs on the wagon lines. We suffered no casualties. Practice alarms were carried out satisfactorily and a full report on them sent to 66th Brigade HQ. Sections on the front line were relieved after the usual tour of front line duty. Further reconnaissance of V sector was carried out. Sections in reserve were given as much training as possible in rifle courses, revolver shooting, firing stoppage. All the guns of the Coy fired at hostile aeroplane at range of 900 to 1400 on various occasions. Apparently, no damage done to enemy plane."

DIARY DURING MY PERIOD IN SALONIKA

"A Taube paid us a visit. Fired about 1000 rounds at him. No luck, so turned my attention to a golden eagle," 14 February 1917

15 February 1917
Lieutenant Greer invited us to Reselli for a little concert. Had quite an enjoyable day.

16 February 1917
Went again to Reselli and in the afternoon Jerry commenced shelling the reserve trenches. We did not think that there would be a digging party of the East Lancashires out and we just said go it Jerry, you are only punching the earth about. Up went the trenches and dugouts blown sky high. But the East Lancashires were there and caught it all having three killed and fifteen wounded. Their commander must have been mad to let the fellows work on the trenches by daylight. So that finished our enjoyment of the day! Hang you Jerry! You will get something for that, you cannot knock our boys about for nothing! We got wind that our guns would open fire at 8:30 p.m. so we made up our mind to watch it where we were building our dugout. At night one can take a chance so we got on top of the dugout and waited.

At 8.30 a.m. sharp the guns opened out and Jerry had the loveliest bombardment. It was a grand sight at the back of us the flash of guns and in front the crash of bursting shells. One cannot imagine it as you look to the rear just behind the hills, the guns were flickering with light as each shell was sent on its way. All you could see was a great number of flashes then a terrifying whirl, then a crash and crump as they burst on the enemy front line and that is what he gets everytime he misbehaves himself.

21 February 1917
Finished the dugouts.

22 February 1917[26]
Nos.3 and 4 guns came up and we commenced our duties in the line. About 200 yards from our dugouts are the front line trenches and in front of this an advanced post - the Rollo section[27].

23 February 1917
Went to Rollo trenches at dusk and have to leave them before dawn as we have to go into no-man's-land to reach them. You dare not stay

---

[26] 66th MGC War Diary, 21 – 28 February, 1917: "Coy HQ and reserve sections were inspected by the GOC 66th Brigade in general turnout and coming into action. They were tested in the latter in supposition that all officers and NCOs had become casualties...Enemy aircraft became more active and the vicinity of the camp of Company HQ and reserve sections were shelled. The fire of the Vickers and Lewis Guns at enemy aircraft was not effective. The commanding officer made frequent inspection of the front line sections. Another section was sent up to the front line to work on the emplacements and dugouts in the BJ line. The laying of the tactical wire was not well done chiefly owing to the fact that the work had to be done on very dark nights and that there was no R.E. supervision or advice arranged for. The commanding officer returned to the Company for duty on the 21st. The health of the Company continued to be good. Special precautions were taken in view of the supposed likelihood of enemy attack about the end of the month...Orders were received on the 28th that the BJ line would be occupied on the 1st."

[27] A series of outposts in advance of the main J Sector line between the ruined village of Reselli and Wagon Hill.

in them during the day as they are only shallow trenches and have no protection at all. There is no shelter at all and it is cold and raining. It was a rotten night, we were almost frozen and hugging against each other for warmth and trying to make a bit of shelter by spreading a groundsheet over the trench and holding it down with mud.

24 February 1917
Everything in ice. Oh! These confounded trenches, snowing all night and all we could do was to try to keep moving about or I am sure we would get frozen stiff. This is a rotten climate and to feel the wind when it comes from north Russia, down the Vardar Valley, is awful. It would cut through sheet iron (I do believe).

February 25, 1917
This morning we had a little canteen stuff up: milk, rolled oats, chocolate and cigs. Fred, Muncey and myself thought that we would like a Dixie[28] of oats to warm our insides. Got the brazier going, filled the mess tin with water, put in the oats and milk. Jove! Did it not look great. (Ah.) They are almost done, our mouths are watering, we have a little taste just to see what it was like. It is a luxury, we will enjoy it. Now we will go and get our spoons and now for our banquet. Crash! What's that? We three run to the entrance of the dugout and to our dismay our lovely porridge is on the ground. The wind had blown over our fire and upset the lot. I felt like crying and by the look on my pals' faces I believe they did. We picked up the mess tin, but it was all gone except that which remained on the sides, so we made the best of that. Still we soon forgot it, as almost everything. The life in the trenches soon makes you forget things.

26 February 1917
Still very cold and snowing.

---

[28] Term used for a soldier's mess tin.

27 February 1917
No.3 gun team caught a Bulgar (or rather he had come to give himself up). He said something about them attacking us on March the 1st.

"Up rolled the infantry and filled the trenches until we could hardly move," 28 February 1917

28 February 1917
Wind up! Out all night fixing up barbed wire behind old wire and in front of new emplacements. Also range finding distances for cross firing and all the other gadgets for machine gun firing. Up rolled the infantry and filled the trenches until we could hardly move.

DIARY DURING MY PERIOD IN SALONIKA

1 March 1917[29]
Everything ready for the enemy attack. He did not come. Hardly a shell over.

2 March 1917
Nothing doing.

3 March 1917
Front line back to normal.

4 March 1917
Took up new position further left called the F10 trenches. Trenches full of mud and it is still snowing. Could not sleep during our time off sentry duty. At 5:30 p.m., Taubes came over and bombed reserves. Six men hit.

5 March 1917
At about 10:30 a.m. this morning, twenty-one Taubes came over. We blazed away at them, but they took no notice and went right over and behind the line and came back at about 11:00 a.m. Heard afterwards that they went to Janes[30] *and bombed the aerodrome. Not much damage. At about 11:00 a.m., another twenty-five Taubes over. What's up? Heard that they went to Salonika Base at Summer Hill. Up to 2000 casualties.*[31] *They caught the poor chaps while on*

---

[29] 66th MGC War Diary, March 1-8, 1917: "Ardzan. The Company remained in the I and J sectors and did a lot of work on the BJ line which was occupied. During this period the enemy shelled our wagon lines and reserve camps frequently, mainly by the help of aeroplane spotting. Much ammunition was fired by the Company. Draft of 9 men arrived who were a good class of men and well-trained. For the first time since landing in Salonika, the Company was up to establishment without having to borrow men from battalions."

[30] Name given by British soldiers to the village of Yanesh.

[31] Here, George is recording one of the bombing raids made by Kaghol 1, a specialist German bomber squadron equipped with AEG, Friedrichshafen, Gotha and Rumpler twin-engined aircraft and its own integrated fighter escort. The unit arrived at Hudova in early 1917 and made its first raid, against a French airfield at Gorgop on 26 February. Subsequent raids were made against forward RFC airfields including Yanesh. The main targets

parade. One batch of 200 were caught just ready for leave and others in trenches training bayonet charging. It must have been hell.

6 March 1917
We are going to be relieved by 60th Division.

7 March 1917
Are relieved but are not going to move off until the 9th, so just unpacked our blankets. The 60th Division boys want to know all about the front. We told them not to take advantage of the Bulgar and all would be easy – only the trenches are rotten!

8 March 1917[32]
Had a very easy day. The 60th Division do not seem to want to take advice; they are wandering all over the place. Well, they will soon learn!

9 March 1917
Packed up blankets and at 10:00 p.m., the mules arrived and we loaded up. At 3:00 a.m. on the 10th we arrived well back from the line at "The Fort," a hill held by the Turks in the last Balkan wars.

---

however were the camps and depots around Salonika. A raid on Summer Hill Camp on 27 February resulted in 300 casualties. Given the close proximity of hospitals to the camps it was inevitable that bombs fell on medical establishments, 29th General Hospital having several men killed on 4 March. The raids were a big talking point in Macedonia and troops up country would have had a clear view of the raiders flying to and from their target. Many rumours spread regarding the effectiveness of the raids and George's mention of a much exaggerated 2000 casualties is an example of this. In May 1917, Kaghol 1 withdrew from Macedonia to take part in raids on London. This was much to the relief of the RFC who, despite Lieutenant Gilbert Ware Murlis-Green bringing down a bomber on 18 March, had little in the way of aircraft capable of taking on and defeating the bombers.

32 66th MGC War Dairy, 8 - 17 March 1917: The Company was relieved by 180th MGC in the line and went into Corps Reserve near GALAVANCI, where they carried out a very extensive and beneficial week's training for offensive operations. The vicinity of the camp was shelled by enemy high velocity guns on two occasions during the week. The weather was very bad and eight mules died.

DIARY DURING MY PERIOD IN SALONIKA

10 March 1917
Up at 7:30 a.m., found out that we were not out for a rest, but to work and practice attack which we have to carry out on a new front. Started at 8:30 a.m., went about umpteen miles with belt boxes, finished 12:30 p.m., done up.

11 March 1917
Same work. Training in attacking in open order by sectional rushes, carrying fighting equipment and two belt boxes. It's hard work.

March 12, 1917
Training again - Went out as infantry attacking in sectional rushes. Got near ravine, 200 yards to go, 'order' came to rush to ravine and take cover. We were all just about fagged out. All we could really do was about 100 yards. One chap fainted, so I had to keep with him, but had to call the assistance of a sergeant as he began to struggle and we had our work cut out to keep him still. Poor chap went unconscious about three or four times in the spell of about half an hour. Had him taken away by Red Cross. I went on guard in the evening and the company had a bit of a concert.

March 13, 1917
Another day of guard. Had to turn out the guard umpteen times. During the day, Jerry bombarded the 60th Division. Thought they would get it before long as they would continue to walk about under the eyes of the enemy.

March 14, 1917
Nothing doing from us but 60th Division retaliated strongly – good boys.

March 15, 1917
Nothing doing during the day. Concert at night (great).

March 16, 1917
Done sham attack. Had to pack up ready for going up line in case 60th Division needed help. It is very cold, rain and sleet.

March 17, 1917
All last night it was blowing a blizzard snow and terribly cold. The wind went down in the morning. We were told to go to the transport. When we got there we had to bury eight mules that had died with the cold, while others had broken their ropes and were all over the plain. Some could not get away, so died and the few that survived had to be untied and kept on the run to prevent them from going stiff. It was a rotten job, burying the mules. When we got back to camp we were ordered to Stand To and when we went to sleep had to do so fully dressed as Johnny was attacking the 60th Division near Lake Ardzan.

18 March 1917
Report that Johnny attacked three times but was repulsed with hundreds dead. Also, in the afternoon, three batches of aeroplanes came over and bombed us with 120 pounders. No one hurt. Moved to new camp nearer line between Gugunci and Rates.

19 March 1917[33]
Did odd jobs. Had first bath for five weeks. Went on guard. Received Mother's photo.

20 March 1917
Very easy day.

---

[33] 66th MGC War Diary, 19 – 31 March 1917: The Company relieved 78th MGC on the front line in D and E sectors with Company HQ and one section at BUJUKLU. One section was put at the HORSESHOE and two at D sector. The relief was shelled in one part of D sector. Casualties: one mule. The Company was very pleased to be in positions near enough to the enemy to be able to use their guns with effect and the change was very good for them as there is no doubt they were getting stale, continually looking at enemy positions 2000 yards away. "Strafes" were worked out and put through nearly every night. We had one man wounded (Private Schofield). A lot of time was taken up by arranging strafes and reconnaissance's of the new area behind and in front of our line. Barrages were registered. The weather became very hot and malaria began to make itself felt again.

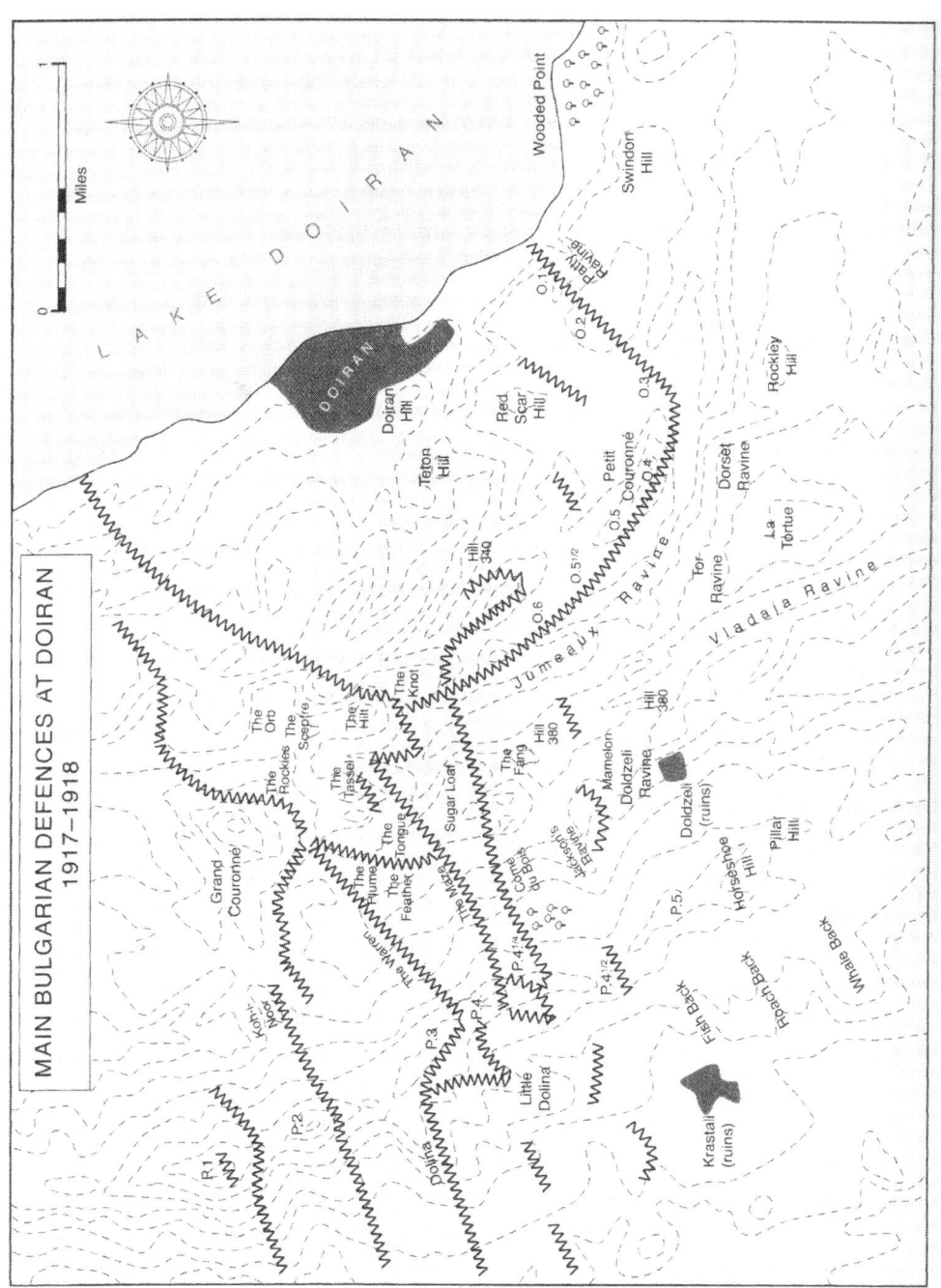

Bulgarian defences at Doiran 1917 – 1918.

21 March 1917
Reveille at 4:00 a.m.. Had a stiff march to another camp nearer the line. Arrived at camp 10:00 a.m. Had a rest then fixed up bivvy.

22 March 1917
Reveille at 8:00 a.m. First parade 9:30 a.m. Got pulled over the carpet for not being quite ready.

23 March 1917
Plenty of work to do. Guard in the evening.

24 March 1917
Up at 6:30 a.m. First parade 9:30 a.m. Had camp orders read out. Training – first, hill climbing with guns, then immediate action, then hill climbing again. After that, gun drill. Then ammunition belt filling. We nearly all fainted (but Hamilton was always an idiot). We then had to find way to new positions in Doiran Front, shell holes everywhere and under observation most of the way. At 5:00 p.m. after our tramp to the front, we had to go help R.F.A[34] get their guns up a stiff incline as the horses would not be able to guide them round the bend properly on account of ravines each side of the road. Some fun. Five of 'em. Hard work dragging 18-pounders about with each weighing 18 hundredweight. Watched a battery of 60 pounders go into action. Then on to Pillar Hill and through a communication trench to the back of Berk's Hill. Had to go along steady though and keep to screened paths as most of the way was under observation from Hill 535 or Dub[35] as it was called. Wherever you went that great hill or mountain if you like to call it seemed to always be looking down on one and up there was the enemy observation point and what a position to hold. If only we were up there and them down in our position. And to the right is Grand Couronné, another bad hill and another one of his observation posts[36] and, I expect I shall see them often in the future.

---

[34] Royal Field Artillery
[35] Bulgarian name for Pip 1 (P1)
[36] Location of the 'Devil's Eye' - name given by British troops to the Bulgarian observation post on the summit of Grand Couronné, from where men of XII

Remains of the Devil's Eye observation post on the summit of Grand Couronné at Doiran.

25 March 1917
Went on fatigue in cookhouse while the other boys had inspection and hill climbing practice. I sat on the opposite hill peeling potatoes and looking at the boys struggling up the hill with the guns and hanging for dear life to the bushes to prevent slipping to the bottom. Jove! The poor chaps had a rotten time of it. But of course I could not cry. I should liked to have done but their antics caused me to smile and think myself dashed lucky that I was peeling potatoes. That was Ham's idea the climbing mountains with guns (but he was always an idiot).

26 March 1917
Went on air picquet. Done nothing else all day. Fred went up the line with his gun team, kept with Charlie.

Corps believed the Bulgarians could observe their every move.

27 March 1917
Cleaned up camp, loaded mules and at dusk we all moved off up to the line. Arrived at Berk's Hill, unloaded the mules and got stuff into dugouts. Got our gun and made off to Position D12 on Horseshoe Hill. It had been raining all day and everything including us was wet through. To get to our position we had to go to the left of Berk's Hill turn into Whizz Bang Ravine or Dead Man's Ravine, whatever you like to call it. The ravine was known by either name. When about 100 yards along we turned into a trench leading up the left side of the ravine and followed this almost to the top of Horseshoe Hill. We splashed through mud and water banging against the side of the trench until we were covered all over in mud. The boys were growling and swearing all the way. On reaching the position, we realized that we had to stand in water or rather a running stream while on duty and it was beastly cold. It's a great life! It's more busy on this part of the line than the Vardar.

28 March 1917
Tried to sleep and dry our clothing. Done some strafing at Johnny and he strafed back with machine gun and rifle fire. The 'Mad Major' in charge of a nearby field battery stopped him arguing with a little shrapnel. Old Fred got 21 days[37] for nothing, also Scotty. Poor old Scofield got a couple of machine gun bullets in him when just turning into Dead Man's Ravine - one in the neck and another in the leg. Always plenty of bullets flying about that ravine.

29 March 1917
Slept all day. Our boys strafed Johnny but it was rather quiet, just a few over at Stand To.

---

[37] Field Punishment

"Oh, you lovely moon, you have given me away!" 30 March 1917

30 March 1917
Johnny strafed us with coalboxes, 5.9 whizz-bangs, rifle grenades, trench mortars and became quite nasty in general. I went on sentry at 10:00 p.m., it was very quiet and a beautiful moon just rising over the top of Horseshoe Hill. Our trench running down the side of the hill and our section was called D.12. I was looking at the moon shining oh so bright and thinking of Blighty and other things, when my thoughts were brought back by a whistle of a bullet and the blighter was near.

So, I took cover for a second, then had a look round. No sooner had my head got just beyond the parapet, when a couple more came. Surely I was not being watched, but I had to look round in case of trouble. I should liked to have kept my head down. But, well, we don't want Johnny on top of us. So, I had another peep, but you could not really call it a peep cuz my head was not up long enough before whistle, whistle. One bullet smashed itself through the parapet, grazing my haversack and hit the other side of the trench. Oh, you lovely moon, you have given me away! Johnny had seen my head against the moon just as it had come over the hill and he was taking pot shots at me. I felt as comfortable as a black kettle on a hot stove. Just at that moment, Ham came along (our dear officer, nice chap, I don't think)!

Me: "Who goes there?" (You have to ask that to Ham or he thinks you are disobeying army orders.)

Ham: "I am Lieutenant Hamilton. How are things here tonight, Burford?"

Me: "Bit quiet Sir. One or two bullets about. I think Johnny has spotted me. Anyway they are sending their shots a bit near."

Hello! Ham gone. Nice fellow, never bothers you much (if you say that bullets are near). When Ham had disappeared, I had just another little peep and I felt a draft at the back of my neck. I just naturally shot my head forward until it nearly touched the parapet and at that moment another draft in between my nose and the parapet. That settled it. He had seen me and getting a bit too near and affectionate, I shifted my position a little further away. Whether he thought he had pipped me I do not know but he turned his attention elsewhere. Relieved at 12:00 a.m. and was not sorry.

1 April 1917
Still getting it thick. Was doing up my putties in the trench when Johnny sent over a rifle grenade and "woof" a piece spun near my ear, so I finished my putties in the dugout doorway. A piece off a coalbox came within a couple of inches from me, so I finished dressing at the back of the dugout. Got relieved by No.3 gun and went back to dugout behind Berk's Hill. In the evening we had to go back to Oxford Run

about 1/2 mile from the line to bring up quadrants[38]. *After a struggle, we were almost in camp. Johnny started sending machine gun bullets about. He could enfilade the valley which we had to go through and we also had to pass Dead Man's Ravine. He was sending them both ways. We could not drop the quadrants because they would need extra men to help us get them down. We had to corner each on our shoulders and if one let go it would have been the devil of a noise. We just had to go on with our hearts in our mouth wondering when one of us was going to ditch but we got through without a scratch. One or two hit the quadrant. It's a rotten corner to pass at any time. Got to bed at about 10:30 p.m.*

2 April 1917[39]
Went out with a different range-finder as my range-finder is in dock. Had to go out beyond our position D12 on Horseshoe Hill. Cadged a cigarette off No.3 gun team and then set to work. Johnny is still sending over all sorts of funny things. Peeping cautiously over the top of the trench I saw a large shell-hole and I could see that I would just be able to slip over the top and into the hole which I did by keeping flat all the while. Once settled I slipped the range-finder very very carefully over the top and got ranges of Mamelon, the Tongue and Sugarloaf and back to dinner. Went out again in the afternoon to take more ranges of Pip Ridge. In bed at 10:00 p.m. Strafed Johnny at 2:00 a.m. on the 3rd.

---

[38] A quadrant is an arched sheet of corrugated iron usually 2 feet 9 inches wide, with the top of the arch standing at 3 feet 8 inches tall. This material was widely used during the First World War in the construction of dugouts, shelters, emplacements, culverts and foot bridges. A number of quadrants could be fixed together to create shelters of varying size.

[39] 66th MGC War Diary, 2 April 1917: I reported at Brigade HQ for further instructions. There was a small raid on the trenches immediately to the left. Enemy trench mortars fire on D Sector in the vicinity of our gun emplacements. Considerable difficulty in getting supplies of good quality small arm ammunition was experienced until I explained the urgent necessity to the OC Ammunitions. Enemy working parties were fired on by night.

"I had just got the range finder in position...when smack a bullet hit the earth in front of my finder and a rifle grenade burst in the trench," 4 April 1917

3 April 1917
Still going about with range-finder taking ranges of Pip Ridge and Doldzeli village. Very hot and feeling fed up. Got back at 12:00 p.m. and had dinner. Tried to get a sleep in the afternoon, but no, Ham wanted me to get some more ranges. Blow the range finder. I also had sentry duty that night, so only got about three hours sleep.

4 April 1917
Same again. Getting more fed up and tired, wish I could get a little sleep. Went out to my point beyond D12 on Horseshoe Hill to take ranges of Tongue and Sugarloaf (we have an idea something is going to happen – one of these fine days. I have not been taking ranges for nothing.) Sergeant Bruce came with me and when we got to the shell hole he said "Is that the place?" "Yes", I said, "I just get into the cut of the trench and slide over into the hole." "Have you been out there?" he asked. "Can you see a better place to take the ranges of the Tongue?" "You don't think I want to crawl into the damned hole if there was

another place do you?" He did not. So we both crawled up the cut and while he remained in the cut, I slid over the tip into the shell hole. Everything had been alright up to today. What he had done I did not know, but I had just got the range finder in position to take a range of the Tongue when smack a bullet hit the earth in front of my finder and a rifle grenade burst in the trench. I did not know if I had been seen or what. All I could do was stay still and wait as nothing else happened and I could hear nothing like it from the sargeant. I gave a quick roll and slid into the cutting then into the trench and I thought Bruce had been hit, but he had not. "Do you think they saw me?" I asked. "I don't know" said he. "I wanted to see how you got the Tongue when he fired." So we guessed that they had seen us. That finished range-finding for the morning, so we returned back to camp and as I expected, I had to go into that rotten hole and take more ranges in the afternoon, so off I went again to D12. Ham's never satisfied. Reached Dead Man's Ravine, when a 5.9 came a bit near. Dived into a disused dugout. Another 5.9 over a bit too near for my liking. Got to D12. Done the job. Got back to tea and on sentry at 8:00 p.m. Got relieved by McQueen and while going down the hill got sniped at so had a run for it. He was using automatic rifle, shots was coming as from a machine gun. Got under cover alright.

5 April 1917
More dodging about with range-finder. In the early evening I had to lead up mules from Oxford Run with ammunition. Johnny turned machine gun on us. Oh, what a life! Finished at 12:00 a.m. Went on sentry until 2:00 a.m.

6 April 1917
Came off sentry after second turn at about 7:00 a.m. and I was hoping for a good sleep. When I do get one I shall sleep until the end of the war if Ham will let me. But no had to go to D.12 again with range finder. Confound it, don't I do enough firing all night and sentry only getting about two hours sleep without going out all day with the range finder. Ham is coming to see me at 12:00 p.m., but did not turn up. Missed six hours good sleep. So I came back to dinner. Ham

wanted me to go out in the afternoon but I got him to understand how I was feeling. I was dog-tired and am not going to do it anymore, so I crawled back to my dugout and fell asleep. Ham let me sleep until 10:00 p.m. and he wanted me to fire on Mamelon from Berk's Hill. After about half an hour of that came back a bit and done sentry. At 10:45 p.m. our boys started a lovely bombardment. Oh what a smash up for the Bulgar. He retaliated and it got a bit too warm, so my No.2 thought it more prudent if we took cover in a shell slit about twenty yards down the hill. So we made a dash for it. Was not very safe, so we decided to get to a dugout a little further down. He shot out of one end and I shot out of the other. I managed to cover about ten yards when I stepped and finished the rest of the journey head over heels and got into a lovely tangle with my rifle and equipment. The strap of my rifle almost strangled me and with the mud that I took with me, I looked a picture. Got to dugout and saw my No.2 with a big grin all over his face as I got out of the entanglement of rifle and kit. Johnny finished a while after so we returned and was relieved at 12:00 a.m. and did some digging until 2:00 a.m., then back to dugout to sleep.

7 April 1917
Went on mess orderly and had an opportunity to sleep. Went on sentry at Stand To and at 8:00 p.m. packed up for going down line. On sentry again at 10:00 p.m., Johnny started to bombard us. Had rather a hot time of it. Had to evacuate position and get in bombproof dugout. It was quiet once again after about twenty minutes. At 2:30 a.m. on the 8th he started up again and we caught other bits of old iron, not so bad as last lot but got snipped at though. I wish I could find the blighter and let him feel a few bullets from my old gun. Word then came round that we are not getting relieved until the 10th after all.

8 April 1917
A bit quiet. Nothing to shout about.

9 April 1917
A bit of firing in the evening just to show Johnny that the 66th are still knocking about. The worst of this business is that one doesn't know

what will happen next. One minute it will be so quiet and the next the whole blooming earth appears to be a quake. Things happen so sudden sometimes it will be almost quiet for two or three days and the next everyone will be on tenter-hooks and everything would be bedlam let loose.

10 April 1917[40]
Finished for a while and got packed up. Transport came at 8:30 a.m. Got mules packed up and ready to move except No.1 & 2 guns and had to wait for them. Of course the transport did not mind waiting! - we could tell that by the things they said about us! They appear like runners waiting for the gun so as to get away. Well, I don't blame them as those mules are none too gentle to handle if a shell bursts anywhere near. So we all got away about 12 p.m. and how quiet everything was. We walked off without a shot being fired. The only night Johnny let us have peace and quiet. But one beastly mule was inclined to make up for things in another direction. I was at the rear when it began to go on strike. He had the blankets and whether he objected to the weight or not I do not know. Lieutenant Eccles[41] told

---

[40] 66th MGC War Diary, 10 - 16 April 1917: Discipline and smartening up parades were held twice daily. There were frequent kit inspections and gas instruction parades. Sports were held and frequent concerts, including one given by the concert troupe 66th Field Ambulance. Canteen stores in great variety were obtained and sold to the men.

[41] Edward Eccles was born on 3 March 1895, the son of a cotton manufacturer, his parents then living at 'Roxley', 29 Demesne Road, Whalley Range, Manchester. Interestingly, on his various service documents, Eccles lists his occupation as 'traveller', 'junior partner cotton manufacturer' and 'shipping clerk'. He joined the 21st Royal Fusiliers as a private on 20 November 1914, going to France with the battalion in November 1915 and serving with the unit's machine gun section. Eccles returned home in March 1916 and joined No.1 Officer Cadet Battalion to gain a commission and on 5 August 1916, he was posted as a 2nd Lieutenant to the 4th Manchesters. However, Eccles would not serve long with his new battalion as he was seconded to the 66th MG Company in Salonika on 3 October. In common with many servicemen in Macedonia, Eccles contracted malaria, being admitted to the 29th General Hospital on 4 June 1917. He rejoined 66th MG Company on 27 July. Whilst serving in Salonika, Eccles put in for a transfer to the Indian

me to tell the mule the error of its ways and to bring him along. I believe he knows I am fond of them. I tried to get out of it by asking "How about my gun?", but it was no use, so I had to go and speak to the brute of a mule. He was stuck at the mouth of Dead Men's Ravine. I felt none too comfortable by the time I got him on the footbridge but at least my pal Charlie was with me as even the transport chaps who could manage the beast better had hurried off. So we had to manage the best we could. "What are we going to do now?" Charlie said. I suggested leaving the beastly thing, but that was more than we dared to. After moving on a short distance the blasted mule suddenly kicked and off shot the blankets. We loaded him again as best we could but it would have made a good transport man weep. One bundle was on his back and the other hanging between his legs tripping him up. Eventually we got everything straightened up and moved off. We were just beginning to enjoy ourselves. Charlie and I spoke nicely to the mule, then almost kissed him, then swore at him, thumped him and then spoke nice again. All the time I pulled at his head while Charlie pushed him from behind. When we did get him to go, it was about 100 yards at a time. Then we saw a streak of dawn across the top of Grand Couronné. Also, in trying to get the mule along we had got off on the wrong track and stood on the 420 Road[42].

Army but later withdrew this application. On 5 February 1918, he gained promotion to Lieutenant. In October, Eccles suffered a second bout of malaria on reaching Bralo whilst on his way back to the UK on leave. Despite this, he reached Southampton on 9 November but with his malaria getting worse was admitted to the Royal Victoria Hospital, Netley on 7 December. Unfit for service due to illness, Eccles had his leave extended. At a medical board on 7 January 1919, Eccles was graded C1 and just over two weeks later the Army decided not to retain him in service. Eccles was demobilised on 5 March 1919.

[42] Track leading from Hill 420 (1 ¾ miles behind La Tortue) to the ruined village of Doldzeli. The track passes east of Castle Hill and Kidney Hill, crosses Boundary Ridge and follows the lower slopes of Pillar Hill and Horseshoe Hill.

DIARY DURING MY PERIOD IN SALONIKA

"I expect the old mule thought he had better be moving; he had heard that noise before, so he ran," 10 April 1917

We knew that if we did not clear, Johnny would see us and perhaps help us along with nothing under a 5.9 and that thought did not comfort us. So, with renewed vigor, we pulled and pulled at the mule. It was almost light now and we prepared for the worst. Just as we decided to clear out the best way we could and leave the mule, a whizz-bang burst behind. I expect the old mule thought he had better be moving; he had heard that noise before, so he ran. Then the excitement and fun commenced. Up the road he tore, I hanging on to the halter and Charlie hanging on to the baggage rope, the blankets shooting this way and that, which caused the mule to go faster. The two of us yelling for all we were worth, rushed up the 420. We cut off up a path on the right leading to Castle Hill with whizz-bangs popping away behind until we reached Castle Hill. There stood some R.F.A. boys cheering and dancing about and quite enjoying the sight of two poor blighters and a mule trying to race whizz-bangs. We came to a halt beside them and while we were getting our breath back, they unpacked and packed the mule for us. We strolled back to camp. I hope I never lead another mule, I'm fed up with 'em.

11 April 1917
In rest camp again. Same old thing, cleaning buttons. Thank goodness we do not have to do them in the line.

12 April 1917
Went for first bath in the last four or five months. Too much water about this place! Meantime, our dirty clothes were being disinfected -- they needed it. While that was being done, we built a sandbag wall across two big rocks through which ran a stream with the idea of making a small swimming pool and the way the water is filling up, it looks good.

Men of the 7th South Wales Borderers enjoying a swim during the summer of 1917. (IWM HU 88193)

DIARY DURING MY PERIOD IN SALONIKA

13 April 1917
Had some sports such as five-a-side footer. Got a kick in the ankle but it did not amount to much. After football, dinner, after dinner went to our homemade pond. Got a long trunk of a tree and put it across the pond. The width of the ravine being only about ten feet wide near the rocks made the water just about wide and deep enough to splash and gamble about in and by putting the tree trunk across the water made a dandy pillar-fight pole and I must say that pole was none too smooth. When one sat astride it and tried to keep on it while being buffeted by the other fellow it made ones legs inside a bit sore. But altogether a good day.

14 April 1917
More sports. Went to our swimming bath but it did not look very inviting. It must be the heat of this place or something but that pond was full of small wiggly things[43]. *It doesn't take long for water in this place to get stagnant if its passage is blocked anywhere and it can't keep flowing, so we soon got sick of it and decided it was not worth taking a dip.*

 Later had clothes disinfected and they wanted it.

15 April 1917
Had rest all day. Went on church parade, the first for two months. Didn't know it was Sunday until we heard about the parade, one hardly knows one day from the other unless something happens like this. I don't think we had a church parade for at least well I don't know when. Anyway, of course got all dressed up and all marched in front of the camp and formed a square around the preacher and he did the usual sermon and we yelled the usual hymns. Got photo of Spanish girl by the name of Peggy Leg (good name that) so wrote to her.

---

43 Mosquito larvae, commonly known as 'wigglers'.

16 April 1917[44]
Got ready for going up the line. I am missing when the mules arrive, it will break my heart if I have to lead another. Marched off at 7:00 a.m. Took over position at 9:00 a.m. Johnny very quiet.

17 April 1917
Not much doing. Johnny sent a few over and the boys sent plenty back.

18 April 1917
Our boys still going strong. Was orderly to Hamilton. We strafed Johnny with our guns from a position just left of Jackson's Ravine. Went on sentry, was taken off to see Ham, back at midnight. Just crossing ravine, when Johnny sent over some whizz-bangs. Had to sit in a wide and shallow trench with a machine-gun behind me and pressing into the back of my neck. Once the firing stopped we dashed across the ravine and up went one of Johnny's very-lights, got spotted so he whizz-banged us a bit more but we got back safe.

19 April 1917
Slept almost all night, went on sentry, got pipped at by a sniper. Had to do mess orderly and was going to draw some water from a spring at the bottom of the hill, when a 5.9 came over and burst about six yards from it, knocking one chap out. He got it in the neck. The Bulgar still sent them near the spring, so we gave it a wide birth and went without water and put up with what we had.

20 April 1917
My gun is a lucky gun! Got orders to strafe Johnny tonight from the position left of Jackson's Ravine. Our artillery had opened a gap in the enemy wire and our job was to keep firing in conjunction with another gun to prevent the Bulgars filling the gap with new wire. Fired 7000 rounds and got shelled twice in the bargain.

---

[44] 66th MGC War Diary, 16 – 20 April 1917: BUJUKLU – The Company relieved the 65th MGC in the front line and carried out final preparation for attack. There were 2 ½ sections in the front line and 1 ½ for support.

DIARY DURING MY PERIOD IN SALONIKA

"My gun is a lucky gun... Our artillery had opened a gap in the enemy wire and our job was to keep firing...to prevent the Bulgars filling the gap with new wire. Fired 7000 rounds and got shelled twice in the bargain," 20 April 1917

21 April 1917[45]
Rested all day. Went out again at night, another 7000 rounds in same spot. Another barrage put on us. Anyway, Johnny has not had the chance to fill the gap up yet.

---

[45] 66th MGC War Diary, 21 April 1917: There was a final conference of COs at Brigade HQ. Wire cutting by the artillery commenced. All machine guns were in position and fired 15,000 rounds during the night at the gaps in enemy wire. An infantry patrol reported that it had been fired at by one of our guns. Inquiries were made and it was found that this was impossible. It is thought that the infantry, through not having experience of being fired over by machine guns, may have made a mistake.

22 April 1917[46]
We went and Stood To a bit early and as soon as it was dark began blazing away for all we were worth. The Bulgars were trying to fill up the gap in the wire. Our boys would be going over, as far as I know, in a day or two and we have been smashing at Johnny for five days now. They smashed back at us. Where we were firing from had been seen by him, so we had to shift our gun and get into the bay of a trench. It was getting hot and furious. The trench was falling in on us and pieces of earth thumping on our backs as we crouched down. Our hearts thumping in our mouths, at least mine was. Suddenly my heart stopped, a big 'un had crashed through the parapet and into the trench right behind me. I discovered next morning that if I had moved back about a foot I could have sat on it. I sat still holding my breath. The fellows gave a sigh of relief, it was a dud. If it had burst, we would all have been blown to bits.

23 April 1917[47]
The same. Nothing but the continual roar of the guns.

---

[46] 66th MGC War Diary, 22 April 1917: Company HQ moved to HORSESHOE HILL. Detailed hours for firing on gaps cut in the wire were arranged with Colonel Bourchier, RFA and Colonel Ward, RFA, by Lieutenant Barnard and myself. The times were so arranged that the gaps were under fire either by artillery or machine guns all and every night until the attack. 30,000 rounds small arms ammunition were fired tonight by 6 machine guns. There was no retaliation. Roughly 80 percent of machine guns in the line were accommodated in bomb-proof dugouts. All guns used luminous auxiliary aiming marks and either blankets or a flash-hider or silencer made by No. 43605 Private Taylor, the company artificer. These later were very effective. An enemy deserter came into HORSESHOE escorted by the infantry.

[47] 66th MGC War Diary, 23 April 1917: The firing on gaps cut in the wire was continued and tracks behind the enemy line that were known to be used were fired on by night. Approximately 30,000 rounds were fired by 7 guns. The enemy used searchlights trying to locate our machine guns, especially those in the D Section. The only parts of the Vickers Machine Guns which did not stand up to the heavy strain of practically continuous firing by night were the fuse springs and muzzle caps of which several were broken and quickly replaced. The guns of section D4 and D2 were continually searched for by the enemy artillery and emplacements were damaged. Lieutenant Eccles

Panorama across the Doiran battlefield in 1918 with Pip Ridge and Grand Couronné on the skyline. Doiran town is on the far side of Lake Doiran.

kept his gun going whenever required. There were a lot of No.4 stoppages owning to defective ammunition. These of course were only of a momentary nature. The guns under Lt. Hamilton in D14 mounted both on and in front of the parapet and also behind the parapet. In each case blankets were rigged around the guns. This together with the rapid changing of the positions of the guns made it more difficult for the enemy to locate our guns. Throughout the operation, Lt. Hamilton and Lt. Eccles showed great calmness and devotion to duty and both often kept me informed by clear intelligent messages of how they were progressing. The guns of which the muzzle caps were broken fired equally well without them when the fuses springs had been adjusted to suit. Considering the probability in the future of muzzle caps being broken it is essential that all ranks receive further training in the rapid adjustment of the fuses springs to the required weight. During the night the trenches of D14 were fired on by a machine gun from PETIT COURONNE and also by a rifleman who appeared to have a fixed rifle. The searchlight referred to above was fixed on for ten minutes by two guns with combined sights. The light went out for two hours. The disadvantage of firing through blanket screens unless in a covered emplacement appears to be that they show up so distinctly to searchlights and flarelights. It was possible to keep all belts filled, even though the amount of firing was so large. This matter, however, required the constant attention of an officer since owing to great fatigue, men employed on such mechanical work are apt to fall asleep unless properly supervised. The necessity of frequently testing all screws and nuts was apparent. Cases occurred of screwed plugs being driven out by the steam, owing to having worked loose. Condenser union screws also worked loose and allowed the intake of steam. For firing on the gaps cut in wire P4 ½ it was found necessary to employ a third gun. This was taken temporarily from the section in Brigade reserve and put under command of 2 Lt. Barnard whose arrangements for cooperation with the artillery and later on, the infantry, were made with conspicuous ability. The telephone wire between Coy. HQ and Brigade Report Centre was cut. This was repaired under shellfire by Captain Jackson and Private Aylward. At daylight on the 24th all the gaps in cut in the enemy wire were found to be unrepaired showing that the combined firing of artillery and machine guns by night had been completely successful.

24 April 1917[48]

---

[48] 66th MGC War Diary, 24 April 1917: During the day the guns in D2, D4, D14 (2), E8 and E10 were laid for barrages A, B and C. Tripod legs were sandbagged down and arrangements made in the emplacements which made it impossible for the guns to fire below their barrage limits, thus ensuring that our infantry would be absolutely free from all danger of being hit. An especially ingenious contrivance was made by the Company Artificer, Private Taylor instructed by 2nd Lieutenant Barnard whereby, by means of an auxiliary backsight and foresight and luminous spots on the wall inside an emplacement, the fire of a gun could be switched on to any desired point with certainty, care and safety to the gunner. All barrages were registered by daylight with good results. Field Clinometers had been previously handed back to ordinance according to the change in AFG10. The absence of these and the fact that few officers were in possession of compasses was much felt. I am in the opinion that a Field Clinometer, range card, night firing base and compass should be part of the equipment of every gun team. Several of my guns have not yet been fitted with elevating and traversing dials. Every gun should be fitted with one of these. New barrels were received from ordinance and put with the guns firing barrage fire."
1900 hours: a hot meal was issued to the company much credit for this due to Lance Corporal Males who did the cooking under shell fire. At the time ordered all troops advancing were in the exact positions allotted to them, the exact role of every machine gunner advancing had previously been carefully explained by Lieutenant Ritchie (since killed) and Lieutenant Grear who was advancing from E and D sections respectively.
2030 hours: The advancing machine guns "went over the top" exactly and in every detail as ordered...and also in accordance with very clear arrangements made with the 13 Manchester Regiment and 8 KSLI by Lieutenants Ritchie and Grear. The gun team under Lieutenant Ritchie all except one man (Lance Corporal McDonald) became casualties when they had gone 300 to 400 yards from E10. Lance Corporal McDonald after tending to the wounded under heavy shell fire returned and reported to Company HQ.
2135-2235 hours: Barrage as ordered...was fired and kept up notwithstanding heavy shelling on our positions and casualties occurring. The teams and officers of these barrage guns showed the upmost devotion to duty and several of them recommended for decorations. News was reported by 2nd Lieutenant Barnard and reported to Company HQ that P4 ½ had been captured and that the gun team under Sergeant Urquhart was in position at P4 ½ and doing excellent work. It is thought that the troops advancing to Horseshoe were located by enemy searchlights as the enemy opened their barrage fire very soon after the searchlight had been on E10 and E8.
2250 hours: Killed and wounded began to be brought into D4 also 1 Bulgar

DIARY DURING MY PERIOD IN SALONIKA

Went in trenches at D14 for attack. As soon as it was dusk, mounted gun in open emplacement on top of the parapet. I am to fire on the Pips, into the

prisoner. 2nd Lieutenant Eccles reported that in D4 for the remainder of the night all was quiet and that, by good luck, he had not then had any casualties. 2255 hours: Lieutenant Hamilton's barrage guns in D14 were subjected to heavy shell fire, but the gunners showed great determination in keeping guns going. It was reported that Mamelon at 2200 hours had been captured and everything had gone according to programme. Fighting was still seen and heard at Hill 380 at 2250 hours. Lieutenant Hamilton reported that at 2210 hours judging by the places where lights were sent from that he thought we had penetrated into Petit Couronné.
2300 hours: The guns under Lieutenant Grear that had advanced to Mamelon were reported to have located the enemy barrage fire which was put behind them. He was able to start digging in at 2150. Private Armstrong showed resource in dealing effectively with enemy who came to be taken prisoner at the same time other enemy were firing on him. A small counterattack on the right of Mamelon about this time was wiped out by our machine gun fire. Lieutenant Grear was in close touch with Captain Jackson, 8th KSLI, from whom he received valuable assistance. Mamelon work shelled at intervals during the night. The infantry who had gone about 150 yards in front of this work escaped this shelling. This would point to the desirability of not putting machine guns actually in captured work unless there is bombproof cover.
2335 hours: Privates Keable and Riddle who had volunteered to go out under shellfire to salvage the wreckage of Lt. Ritchie's gun team and if possible to bring in wounded and dead, returned to Company HQ bringing the gun and spare parts. They reported that the majority of the remainder of the equipment had been destroyed by shellfire. Private Keable, though wounded in the face, had to be forced to go the aid post as he volunteered to go out again.
2400 hours: Casualties (2) were reported from E8. My message to CT 40 was returned by Brigade HQ as not understood. The message had been read to two officer's before dispatch to make certain that the meaning was clear. Lieutenant Hamilton reported that he thought Petit Couronné was in enemy hands. Lance Corporal McDonald, Lance Corporal Cavanagh and Private Ballantine left HQ to bring in the wounded-dead of Lieutenant Ritchie's gun team and if possible some more gun equipment. They were all volunteers. P 4 ½ was reported to be counterattacked. The counterattack is thought to have suffered heavily from the fire of Sergeant Urquhart's gun at P4 ½ and the guns of Lieutenant Barnard at E8 and the 65th MGC behind the Whaleback. Throughout the night, machine guns fired their barrage in cooperation with the artillery whenever barrages were called for by the infantry.

saddle of Pip 4 ½ and keep up a continual fire swinging the gun slightly to right towards Pip 3. We had fixed up this position a few days ago, fixing up the barrage fire line with cross members of wood that would prevent the gun being lowered too much to prevent the fire hitting our boys as they advanced. At 6:00 p.m., things opened all out - crash, bomb, bang, wallop, whizz, shriek, crash and the tut-tut-tut of the old gun and the whir of small shells. The shriek of the larger is beyond explanation. What with our own guns and Johnny's, well to be in it is to know what it was like. We kept it up for three hours. The old gun was tut-tutting away for all she was worth and spitting out flame and bullets as fast as she could. At 9:30 p.m., the boys went over, we covering them with our fire. They got Johnny's first line, but not Petit Couronné and that spoilt it. It was rotten luck. The reason is this: the East Lancashires, Cheshires, and Manchesters took their part, which was Pip 4 ½, Mamelon, Sugarloaf, while the Worcestershires and Gloucestershires were to take Petit Couronné. They had to go through Jumeaux Ravine, and if ever there was a hellhole, it was that. The concussion of the shells in the confined space of the ravine caused as many deaths as those who were hit by shells. The Worcestershires went first and Gloucestershires followed, but were held back in the ravine. The Worcestershires drove Johnny out and got the place, the Gloucestershires upon getting to Petit Couronné mistook them for the enemy and bombed them. As soon as Johnny saw what was happening he came back and drove them both off. They were fighting right 'til dawn on the 25th and had to retire back to their own line.[49] *All night long it was shelling, shelling, shelling and what with the flashing of guns and the enemy's searchlight playing all over the place one could see almost every hill ravine and valley that we were fighting for. Come dawn the boys were still holding onto their objectives, except Petit Couronné.*

---

[49] George is mistaken regarding the attack on Petit Couronné as this was actually undertaken by the 10th Devons from 79th Brigade. The 11th Worcesters and 9th Gloucesters advanced across Jumeaux Ravine to the left of Petit Couronné to assault positions known as O5 ½ and O6. These attacks failed as did that of the 10th Devons, the unit suffering heavy casualties in its assault on Petit Couronné, the key point in the Bulgarian front line position at Doiran. For a full account of the First battle of Doiran, see *Under the Devil's Eye*' by Wakefield and Moody, p.73-97.

DIARY DURING MY PERIOD IN SALONIKA

April 25, 1917[50]

---

[50] 66th MGC War Diary, 25 - 26 April 1917: "Very little is known definitely about the action of the gun which went forward with Lieutenant Lloyd (KSLI) bombing party. It was reported to have retired at one time and later to have been ordered back into position by Lieutenant Eccles. A court of inquiry was held as the reasons for retirement and the proceedings were sent to HQ 66 Infantry Brigade. Little is known definitely of the gun team under 2nd Lieutenant Moore which went at VLADAJA Ravine behind the Trench Mortar Battery. Thought that it reached its allotted position and did not retire, although it is believed that all the infantry at 380 and the bombing party had retired. During the enemy counterattack on 380 on the 25th, this gun ably handled by Lance Corporal Potter put out of action several enemy in and near 380. Lieutenant Grear at MAMELON found at dawn that one of his positions did not give the required field of fire and shifted his gun to another place. The wire between D14 and company headquarters broken during early morning. Captain Jackson and Private Aylward repaired this wire under shellfire. One gun was moved from E8 to E10 to avoid heavy shell fire. A gun team under Sergeant Thomson was sent out to take the place of the gun team of Lieutenant Ritchie on P 4 ½. They reached the position without casualties and reported having done so. Consolidation of guns which advanced was continued. My section commanders report that they saw no waving of flags at dawn to denote position of advanced troops as had been ordered. About midday the artillery responded to a call for barrages and the machine guns joined in. I imagine in reality this barrage call was put up by the enemy in imitation of signals. MAMELON and 380 was subjected during the day by shelling of all kinds of guns and also by trench mortar. The enemy counterattacked 380 about 1845 was seen and fired on by guns in D14 and VLADAJA RAVINE. The answer to the barrage signals, guns in D14, D4, D2, opened barrages B and C. In response to urgent demands for ammunition from P4 ½ and MAMELON, several boxes small arms ammunition were sent up, although it became necessary to take some gunners away from barraging guns. Two of our own machine guns were put out of action during the night. Ordinance was at once informed and arrangements made to use Lewis Guns until the Vickers were got into action again. Constant communication was kept up between No.2 section at MAMELON and No.1 at D14. During the night Lieutenant Hamilton received several verbal and unintelligible messages from the infantry on his right, which he ignored, excepting that he told the messengers to go and get clear messages. The retaking of P4 ½ by the 13th Manchester Regiment was to a large extent made possible by the action of the gun team under Sergeant Urquhart, who caused many casualties to the enemy. Lieutenant Grear reports that at MAMELON one of the flash-hiding screens fell down and it soon became clear

Shelling occasionally on both sides. The enemy counterattacked at 8:00 p.m. We rushed to our open emplacement under a creeping barrage put down by the Bulgars. Another rotten time of it, but enemy was repulsed with heavy losses.

"Poor old Georgie, the agony on his face…Well, I'll go back to Blighty. But he will never see Blighty again," 26 April 1917

---

to him from the attention this emplacement received from enemy artillery, that the gun had been located. He changed positions.

0700: A message was received from C-in-C that new lines would be held at all costs. That was repeated to sections.

0710: Message from Lieutenant Grear asking for brandy and saying they were carrying on all night. Various messages from Lieutenant Hamilton and 2nd Lieutenant Eccles showing clearly what they thought was the progress of events. During the night one gun in D2 was moved to C20 taken off its barrage duty and put in a position to enfilade the wire from D Sector to the right of 380. 78th MGC were asked to cooperate in protecting our right flank which they agreed to do. During the evening there was an alarm that the enemy was making a general counterattack. This was caused mainly, I think, by enemy systematically shelling our front line and then putting barrage behind the front line. The gunners at Mamelon suffered greatly by having to stand continually in water. Three men afterwards went to hospital with trench foot.

DIARY DURING MY PERIOD IN SALONIKA

26 April 1917
Rather quiet until half past 6:00 p.m. when the enemy counterattacked in daylight. What excitement! We did not know what had happened until we saw our boys coming into our first line from captured trenches without kit and rifle. Then we realized that Johnny was after them. But the R.F.A. soon spotted it and opened out. Back went the boys and got the captured Johnny first line again. But no sooner had our officer seen what had happened when he yelled ACTION! Up went the gun on my shoulder and I had about 200 yards to run to the emplacement. We got there after a good push through the trenches where our boys were packed like sardines, yet a moment before the trench was almost empty. Just after came Georgie McWilliam with the tripod. "Same place Georgie?" I said to him, "No, put it on the front of the trench." So, we stood on the firestep and fixed the gun up on the front. Things were humming with the usual crash-crash. Ten minutes had not passed when crash! Up went our emplacement where we had been going and, if we had put the gun there, we would have been no more. Just then our officer came along and sat on the fire step. "Well, how are things? Rotten, eh?" he said. "You fellows take five minutes each helping the infantry to look out." So Georgie got up for his five minutes by orders of the officer. While he was looking over, I filled my pipe and was talking to the officer and saying that Johnny would not be able to pass the 66th MGC, when a shell found our tripod, smashing the gun and flinging it into the trench just as I was lighting my pipe. I did not hear the crash but saw the flash under my tin hat, so I ducked. Georgie went over with the gun and finished up in the bottom of the trench, sitting with his back up against the old gun. Poor old Georgie, the agony on his face. We lifted him and laid him on his side and took off his jacket and ripped his shirt open and saw about half a dozen pieces of shell in his shoulder and back. And, not a word did he say except "Well, now I'll go back to Blighty." But he will never go back to Blighty again. We dressed his wounds but poor old Georgie died shortly after.[51] *I picked up the*

---

[51] In this instance, George's use of the phrase 'died shortly after' is used to indicate that his friend died days rather than minutes or hours after he was hit. The CWGC records George McWilliam's date of death as 7 May 1917. The

wreckage of the gun and took it to our dugout. (I have kept the fuse spring as a souvenir as that old gun had done its work). In the evening it was quiet and we had to wait for a gun. Told we were going to have a Lewis until a replacement Vickers can be sent up. At about 8:30 p.m., Sergeant Bruce took me off to go to advanced captured trenches to take rations and rum up to Lieutenant Grear's gun. I was just about fed up, tired and feeling pretty groggy. So I went and saw Eccles about it, but he said, "Will you go?" So I just went, got my No.3 to help with the rum and rations and off we went over the top, through the barbed wire and got our bearing. It was pitch dark and could not see anything until we stumbled across a water drum and some belt boxes so we knew that we were on the track of our boys. Got another 100 yards into No Man's Land when up went a Very light so we dropped down and kept still. A whizz-bang came over, but they had not seen us.

The light gave us our bearings and in front of us were more belt boxes, cleaning rods and spare parts which the boys had dropped in the scramble after Johnny. Finding these was a great help and we walked over to our left into a ravine and up to the end and waited to see if we were still all right. We did not know whether Johnny was in front or behind. Then quite near us, up shot a Very light. Luckily, we were laying down so we were able to take a look round and were sheltered by the rocks. Just on our left we saw what we made out to be Grear's position. As soon as we were pretty certain that it was safe to move, we advanced toward it. Just as we were near a sentry yelled out "Halt! Hands up!" but I could only put up one hand because the other held the bottle of rum. So, the voice said "Up with the other hand or I'll blow your bloody brains out." I replied that if he did so they'd lose the rum. This was all they wanted to hear so they pulled us into the trench and took us to Lieutenant Grear. We told him we had rum and wanted to ascertain his position for sending up further rations. After that we hurried back to our lines and as we pretty near knew the way, we did not stop. When we got near our wire, Johnny sent up a Very light and sent a couple of shots and whizz-bangs. So we made a dash

---

fact that he is buried in Mikra cemetery close to Thessaloniki indicates he was transported to a base hospital and died of his wounds.

for our trenches and fell in them. No thankful job fiddling about over the top trying to find gun teams. No new gun yet.

"It was raining lovely and the steam at the bottom was a bit of a torrent," 27 April 1917

27 April 1917[52]
We commenced a barrage at "Stand To" this morning, but it only lasted about two hours. At about 10:00 a.m., Fred Farthing came over with his gun and said that he had to remain. Being his gun, I took

---

52 66th MGC War Diary, 27 April 1917: Frontline battalions relieved by 65th MGC. Gunners not relieved. During the relief Lieutenant Barnard reports that P4 ½ was shelled and that the relieving infantry were short of both bombs and SAA. He could not find the relieving Company Commander for some time. Captain

position No.2 but he said that he was No.2, so I took my usual No.1 position. Just after lunch, I was told that Ham wanted me as I knew the position of the guns out in the front. He knowing jolly well that I went last night and he wanted me to show him the way. It's a wonder, him wanting to go out on top and in the daylight. But he had to go. What for? Goodness knows, as we could not go from the point we went from in dark. We had to go down the trench into Jackson's Ravine and crawl along that. It was raining, lovely, and the stream at the bottom was a bit of a torrent. Most of the way we had to walk through it. We got to the end of the ravine but could not get any further as we would come under observation from Grand Couronné and Pip Ridge. Ham wanted the direction so I told him that the only way was to cross the open space and cut off to the left. He said "Shall we make a dash for it?" I told him it was not worth it. It was certain we would be spotted and Johnny would have smashed us in a second. So we tried to get over a bit of hill which was thick with bushes and the noise and movement caused trying to get through was just as risky. So we laid down in the wet ravine and finally he decided we should leave it until it was dark. We then crept back into our trenches. While Ham went and changed his clothes for dry, I had to let mine dry on me.

28 April 1917[53]
Rather quiet, looking forward to getting relieved. Went to dugout behind hill with all blankets tied in bundles. Sat on one bundle talking to Fred when some shells came over. I darted into the dugout and from the

---

Jackson volunteered to take rum, cigarettes and other stores to P4 ½ and see that all was well with Lieutenant Barnard and Sergeant Thomson's gun.

[53] Unit Diary, April 28, 1917: The enemy artillery, including 8-inch guns, systematically pounded the majority of the places in both lines where our machine guns were. It appears evident that (1) the majority of guns have been roughly located, (2) the fire of our machine guns have done considerable damage. E10 was very much damaged and two of our machine guns in this work were completely buried, they being afterwards retrieved. The Company (less one section) were relieved by the 65th MGC under quiet conditions and withdrew to BUJUKLU. On arrival it was found that owing to casualties there were not enough men to get all equipment back from P4 ½ and MAMELON. Carrying porters were necessary.

opening, old Fred was sitting on the blankets smoking his pipe. "Cripes, Fred, what's the matter with you? Balmy?" I said. And, his remark was "if you are going to be hit, you'll be hit." How true. This is what happened before the day ended. We were packed up and ready when at 2:00 p.m. the enemy put up barrage on the captured trenches. It was hellish. At 5:00 p.m. he put it on our old front line and reserve. At 7:00 p.m. Johnny came over and we got into action. I picked up the tripod and darted for the open emplacement at the top of the trench, Fred following me with the gun when a big 'un burst on the side of the trench. Yelled to see if Fred was alright and then saw him coming through the smoke. Up on the top we went. Got the tripod up and the pins ready to put in, just as Fred placed the gun in position on the tripod he was hit by a piece of shrapnel killing him instantly.[54] I believe I went mad. I dragged Fred into a slit trench and went back into the trench for another No.2. Nobody to be found only me and chap who did not understand the gun. Then up the trench came Lieutenant Eccles. "Farthing knocked out!" I yelled to him. "Can't you find another No.2?" he asked. "Can't find anybody," I yelled. "Where's Corp. Fiddy?" "Damned if I know,'" I yelled back. "Find him!" he shouted. So I went to find him and shouted his name down the trench until my throat was sore. All of a sudden a head popped out of the hole. "Seen Corp. Fiddy!?" I yelled. "Yes, that's me." "Well up on the gun, you have orders!" He did not like it. Anyway, up we went and got the gun going. Could not see for the smoke and bursting of shells and shrapnel. I knew 'Big Lizzie' was trying to find our gun by the burst of the big shells near but she was not quite near enough, thank goodness. Old Fiddy did not know much about the gun and luckily after ten minutes an officer took him away and sent me Thurlow a real No.2. Then we let things rip. I sang, swore and wished Johnny everything. But to sing 'Take me back to Blighty,' well I must have been mad. Whilst this was going on there was one instance that made us smile. A Lancashire fellow who was attached to our gun took a short cut in front of my gun when returning for more ammunition. Just as he went back and taking the short cut, I fired a

---

54 CWGC records Fred's date of death as 29 April 1918, which could well indicate an administrative error on the part of either 66th Machine Gun Company of the Commission.

short burst and he had five bullet marks down the length of his nose, I saw it afterward, five little chips out from the tip to the bridge. It's a good job he was not a bit faster or the poor chap would have got them through the head! Well we got relieved by the 65th Brigade at about midnight and got to camp by 4:00 a.m. on the 29th.

29 April 1917[55]
Rested all day and we wanted it.

30 April 1917[56]
Went on air picquet. Saw old gun that was all smashed up. I was sorry for it and checked up on spare parts lost during attack.

31 April 1917
Packed up for going little further down the line near Three Trees and arrived in the afternoon.

---

[55] 66th MGC War Diary, 29 April 1917: "Lieutenant Moore took a party to MAMELON to search for lost kit and equipment and managed to recover about half of it. The company who were utterly worn only rested."

[56] 66th MGC War Diary, 30 April 1917: Notes: I reported personally at Brigade HQ everyday to give a situation report and to ask for fresh orders. Mules were brought up every night with small arms ammunition and various comforts. The following is a brief summary of the conclusions I have come to and the lessons to have learnt from the operation.
That the establishment of MGC is too small by at least 30.
That with the existing establishment carrying parties are essential (some were unofficially obtained).
That signalers and other ranks require much more training in messages.
That Lewis Guns, rather than Vickers should go with such parties as bombers.
That more use should be made of well-registered overhead indirect fire by day and night.
That Vickers Guns, if properly looked after, will stand a tremendous amount of almost continuous fire. (Approximate total expenditures of SAA by 12 guns was 180,000 rounds (some guns fired as much as 40,000 rounds).
That a flash-hiding contrivance is essential.
That all machine gunners should be trained as bombers.
That it is very useful to establish a dump of canteen stores and to have a good supply of brandy and whiskey to replace rum which did not arrive.
That metal belt boxes are infinitely superior to wooden ones.

DIARY DURING MY PERIOD IN SALONIKA

1 May 1917
Returned gun lent during attack to its original gun team. Got what was left of my old gun together ready to be exchanged for new one.

2 May 1917
Cleaned up everything including ourselves for inspection.

3 May 1917
Got gun, tripod and rest of things exchanged for new.

4 May 1917
Inspection by divisional general and got the usual 'soft soap' about the good work during attack.

5 May 1917
Inspection by Monty Bates.[57] Had look over new gun. Fired it, it's a beauty. Went for a dip in our pool.

6 May 1917
Had clothes disinfected, bath and after that church parade.

7 May 1917
Went to get stuff from E.F. Canteen[58], nothing much about.

8 May 1917
Came over ill at 10:00 a.m. Had to fall out of parade. Ill all day.

9 May 1917
Reported sick and sent to 35 Casualty Clearing Station with tonsillitis and bad head.

---

[57] Brigadier General F S Montague-Bates, commander of 66th Brigade.
[58] Expeditionary Force Canteen: the forerunner of the Navy, Army and Air Force Institute (NAFFI). The EFC ran canteens for British servicemen in all major theatres of war during the First World War.

10 May 1917
Saw another doctor. He said he would keep me in for a day or two. Jolly fine place and a nice bed, clean sheet and good grub.

11 May 1917
Saw the Doc again. Sent down to the 28th General Hospital at Salonika. What a change to the line everything spic and span. I'm going to have a rest and be clean for a while and I am not going to write more until I go up to the line again.[59]

---

[59] During the period George was in hospital and convalescing, his company was engaged with a typical round of work with turns in and out of the line. In May, sections were busy firing on gaps in the Bulgarian wire at night to prevent repair parties undertaking work. The gaps on P4 were a particular target. In retaliation the Company emplacements were shelled. This task was kept up until the end of the month. On 16 May, Lieutenant Wood showed great calmness in extinguishing a fire in the frontline caused by a box a flares being hit by a shell. The month also saw an increase in sickness levels within the Company as many old malaria cases began suffering renewed attacks.

On 2 June, the Company was relieved by 65th MGC and went into camp at Three Trees Fountain. Here much time was spent on improving camp hygiene and sanitation with very satisfactory results. The Company spent the rest of their time engaged in training and smartening up. Sports, especially football and boxing were popular pastimes and concerts were also put on during the month. In addition, the Company was inspected by XII Corps MG Officer and Assistant Directors Medical and Veterinary Services, as well as the commanders of 22nd Division and 66th Brigade. It is also recorded that the Company had only half its compliment of officers. On 26 June, 66th MGC went back into the line taking over E, F and H Sectors. This is a large area for a single company to hold and all guns were in the firing line. All gun teams under instruction not to open fire unless forward infantry outposts are overrun. Much time is spent attempting to establish better machine gun positions.

July saw a complete reorganisation of the machine gun defence scheme of 66th Brigade. The new plan aimed at moving all the guns out of the frontline and other positions occupied by the infantry. For the new emplacements there was to be greater reliance on concealment rather than protection against shell fire. The lack of officers in the Company made itself felt as it proved impossible to relieve officers from the line when sections were rotated. On the night of 30-31 July, 66th MGC were relieved by 65th MGC and returned to Three Trees Fountain.

DIARY DURING MY PERIOD IN SALONIKA

16 July 1917
Discharged from camp and sent to Summer Hill. No sooner there than I was picked for draft to go up the line. Marched to Dudular station, entrained at 5:30 p.m. Almost at Corsika when we got shelled. Reached Corsika at 9:30 p.m., marched to Gugunci, got in bed at 10:30 p.m. Back to the noise of gunfire again!

17 July 1917
Medical inspection. Went to company transport at 5:30 p.m. in the afternoon.

18 July 1917
I am to keep with the transport until going into trenches next time with my Section as they are coming out in a couple of day's time. Don't mind the transport, but oh those mules. Johnny is sending over some big 'uns onto hill beside us. So long as he does not alter range, don't mind so much.

19 July 1917
Helped in stables, at least that is what they called it. Took horses to water and made myself generally useful. Went at night to help bring company out of trenches.

20 July 1917
Told to take mules to grazing ground over by Gugunci, five of em. Well I had to let the transport fellows see that I was enjoying myself and that I had lived with mules all my life, so I got on one bare back and off we went. But it was a sore job. They are too confounded bony for me. Brought them back at 4:30 p.m.

21 July 1917
Old Ham claimed me back in the company. Ham said that the transport was for the duds and he was not going to have any gunners in it. Wonder what the transport would say to that.

22 July 1917
Started with an inspection.

23 July 1917
Inspection and gun drill.

24 July 1917
In training for divisional sports. Company officers to pick out gun team.

25 July 1917
Company picked out No.4 section. They are welcome to the job.

26 July 1917
Inspection again, then went on fatigues.

27 July 1917
Still on fatigues.

28 July 1917
Went in for a little boxing, three hours of it under Corporal Freeman. Went to headquarters as orderly in the afternoon. Three boys from the old regiment, Royal Fusiliers, who were attached to the 10th Division when we came out were left behind by the 10th when they left Salonika, so they were attached to us. There was some rejoicing when we met again.

"Went in for a little boxing. Three hours of it under Corporal Freeman," 28 July 1917

DIARY DURING MY PERIOD IN SALONIKA

29 July 1917
Went to the boxing-ring again.

30 July 1917
Ditto. I think I will wait awhile before I write again.[60]

1 October 1917[61]
Same. Down to the ring.

---

60 For the two month period in which George appears to have kept no dairy the 66th MGC War Diary fills in some of the blanks. The first half of August in spent in camp at Rates with the Company training (including field and night firing exercises), smartening up and engaging in a variety of recreational training, mostly sports, which the CO states was very beneficial and enjoyed by the men. By the end of this training period all sections were at a high state of efficiency despite there being only five officers with the unit. During this time the Company finished second in the 66th Brigade Boxing Championships. The CO puts this commendable performance down to the popularity of the unit's boxing class, volunteers training during the hours reserved for PT. Between 17 and 31 August, the Company is back in the line, taking over a complicated and large sector from 67th MGC. As many infantry battalions had begun receiving their full complement of 16 Lewis guns every effort was made to take the Company's Vickers guns out of the frontline trenches. Typical work carried out during this time was the strafing of Bulgarian communication trenches and working parties. The final few days of the month saw the Company supporting minor operations by 66th Brigade and working with the artillery to lay down fake barrages and bombardments on selected positions to make the Bulgarians think an attack was imminent. The Company was still in the line during the first half of September, continuing with the types of work carried out the previous month. High levels of sickness led to men being attached from the infantry and some firing work being undertaken by infantry Lewis gun sections. All the Company's Vickers guns were moved into emplacements 100 – 200 yards behind the frontline. On 12th and 20th September the Company supported daylight raids by 8th KSLI on O6 and Petit Couronné respectively. During the night of 20 – 21 September the Company was relieved by 65th MGC and returned to Three Trees Fountain camp. After two full days of rest the men began recreational training and smartening up. Further attachments of men joined the unit bringing the Company almost up to full strength.

61 66th MGC War Diary, 1 - 6 October 1917: The training of the company continued while in reserve. The majority of the training consisted of

2 October 1917
Ditto.

4 October 1917
Played footer. No.1 Section vs. No.2 Section. Draw 2-2. Anyway, they did not beat us. Nothing to do rest of the day.

5 October 1917
Went to transport for pack saddles for going up the line. Done at 10:00 a.m. Went up to trenches by my lonesome at 8:00 p.m. to look over new position that I had to take over. New position known as E13 and nearer to Petit Couronné. Saw new emplacement and got what information I needed from the boys holding the position. Was there about 5 minutes when a H.E. came over. Being on top of the trench, I naturally fell in it and chipped my knees in the process. Back in Headquarters by 10:00 p.m. Reported to Ham and went to bed.

6 October 1917[62]
Went up to the line again in the morning, looked over the ammunition and stores. Signed all correct and stayed the day with the 67th Brigade,

---

transport training and reorganization in accordance with verbal instructions received from the Corps Machine Gun Officer, 12th Corps, recreational training in accordance with SS 137 (OB1211a), and preparation for Horse Show. The company received instruction in company drill with pack transport. Officer riding classes were held. The health of the troops again improved, largely owing to the amount of rest they were able to get. A revised SALONIKA 4, G1098, having been received, a lot of time was spent in checking ordinance stores, returning some and drawing or redrawing others. The loading of various mules was reorganized. The company, owing to the number of men allowed to be attached from battalions, was still under strength. Nearly all men attached from battalions applied, after a month or so, for transfer to the Machine Gun Corps. Experiments were carried out with flash blinders, barrage frames, barrage boards and special mountings, which had been invented by Captain Jackson, Company Sergeant Major Simms and Private Taylor and constructed in the company. These experiments showed the inventions, for the most part, to be entirely satisfactory.

62 66th MGC War Diary, 6 – 31 October 1917: The company relieved the 67th MGC in the left subsector without incident. The transport took over the lines of the

whom we are relieving. Section arrived at 7:30 p.m., relieved the 67th Brigade. No.1 gun came to E.13 Section and my gun went to D.8 Section at Berk's Hill when it ought to have been No.1 gun at D.8 and my gun at E.13. So, of course, there was a row, I wanting to know what they were doing in E.13. But they said that Ham had changed it round and that I had to remain with them until Ham came along. Ham can never find me a soft spot. Carried ammunition to emplacement and carried on. Ham came along and said I was to return to my own gun next day.

7 October 1917
Stood down at 5:00 a.m. Got over hill to dugout and went to report to Ham. He dismissed me but wanted to see me at 10:00 a.m. Went to my own gun. Felt sick so kept to dugout. No sentry duty tonight.

8 October 1917
Reported sick. Got L.D. (Light Duty) but went on sentry. Got gun mounted about 10:00 p.m. and was talking to Corporal Gaunt just as Ham came along.
   Ham: "Corporal Gaunt."

65th MGC. The guns of the company fired harassing fire every night from the D, E and F Sectors. Average expenditure of ammunition 2500 per night. It is thought this fire was effective especially in the D and E Sectors, as the enemy began to do the same thing to us, especially on the paths and tracks behind E Sector. The company won 1st prize in the Divisional Recreational Training Meeting, 1st prize for team turnout at the Divisional Horse Show, 4th for pair of pack mules at the Divisional Show and 1st prize for Company Commander Chargers. A large amount of work was done in making emplacements splinter-proof, dugouts bombproof, and in organizing the MG positions in the second line. Trench logbooks were issued for the first time to the company and found invaluable. The health of the company was very good indeed, mainly owing to the change for the better in the climate conditions. Though small drafts arrived they were largely composed of men who had previously been in the company and gone to hospital. In several cases, they did not appear to have entirely regained their health. Working parties were detailed from the infantry transport in the large amount of digging work to be done. They gave very good help to the company.

Gaunt: "Sir"
Ham: "All correct here?"
Gaunt: "Yes, sir"
Ham: "Let me see." Looks at his wrist watch. (A habit of his every time he has to say something).
Gaunt: "Yes Sir."
Ham: "Did you do the digging and bring up the water?"
Gaunt: "Yes, sir".
Ham: "Burford, fire the gun at 12:00 and have it trained on Hill 380 in bursts of 20 to 35 rounds. Muncey will fire in conjunction with you".
Me: " Very good, sir. Gun all ready." – Ham had already given me these orders hours ago!
Ham: "Corp, issue order to gun teams to do day sentry."
Gaunt: "Yes, sir."
Ham: "All stand to in case of attack on 380" (As if we did not know it) "and you most do so and so" (anything to keep us always at it and have no peace at all and that's a fact).
Charlie had a burst at midnight and I finished the firing, but there was really no need for it.

9 October 1917
Charlie and I went on day sentry in the morning. Saw raid on Petit Couronné by the Jocks at 9:30 a.m. soon over.[63] It's a shame to send the boys up on Petit in the daytime. Waste of lives. Johnny sent some big 'uns over at 12:00 p.m. Went on sentry at night. Rather quiet. One of Johnny's machine guns enfiladed our trench and made it a bit uncomfortable.

10 October 1917
Went on lookout in afternoon, quiet until 4:30 p.m. when Johnny started shelling Tortoise Hill and Exeter Ravine. He kept it up until

---

[63] This appears to be a case of mistaken identity by George as the Scottish battalions of 77th Brigade (26th Division) were at this time holding I and J Sectors west of Pip Ridge towards the River Vardar meaning this raid must have been undertaken by infantry from 22nd Division.

Stand To then put isolated ones over for an hour. Then put up a couple of barrages over.

11 October 1917
Quiet all day except for a few shells our boys put over. Ham came 'fault finding.' Not much sleep today.

12 October 1917
Started to rain in the morning. Johnny sent some shells over onto Tortoise Hill. Rained all night, not much cover so got wet and had no sleep. Johnny put up a barrage. Stood to, thought it was a raid, but no.

13 October 1917
Still raining. Storm broke at night. Trench filling with water. Johnny started traversing a machine gun round our position, another rotten night.

14 October 1917
Went to headquarters in morning for rations. Weather clearing up. Sunny in afternoon. Stood To at 6:15 p.m. About 9:30 p.m. up comes fussy Ham and starts his 'fault finding' again. Wants to know what digging we had done. Being rotten weather the last two days or rather nights (we do not do trench digging by day) we did not bother about it. He said: "You must do some until 11:00 p.m. or 12:00 a.m." Old Gaunt said that with doing day sentry and night as well, we were getting fagged out with hardly any sleep at all. Then Ham said that we do nothing but sleep and he is going to see that we get less of it. He had better go easy or he will be causing trouble.

15 October 1917
Went on day sentry getting relieved at 9:30 p.m. tonight. Back at headquarters at 12:00 p.m.

16 October 1917
Done mess orderly, nothing much else to do except two hours digging tonight. Finished at 7:00 p.m.

17 October 1917
Inspection by CO of guns and ammunition.

18 October 1917
Went to Scratchbury Hill to build some dugouts. Back by 11:00 p.m.

19 October 1917
Easy day. Guard at night.

20 October 1917
Went to transport in the afternoon and our boys commenced a five day bombardment for a big stunt.

21 October 1917
Began to rain. Kept on all day. Artillery still going strong.

22 October 1917
Nothing but the Boom-Boom of the guns and crash of explosives and plenty of rain.

23 October 1917
Still raining. Boys still smashing away (that's the stuff to give em, plenty more to come, Johnny!). Am going up line tonight. We relieved No.3 section at 8:30 p.m. Rain left off during night.

24 October 1917
Day turned out fine. Our position is on Claymore Hill. It is thick with bushes but during the day we have to leave gun and get behind hill as the slightest movement amongst the bushes in daylight might be seen. Rain again all night.

DIARY DURING MY PERIOD IN SALONIKA

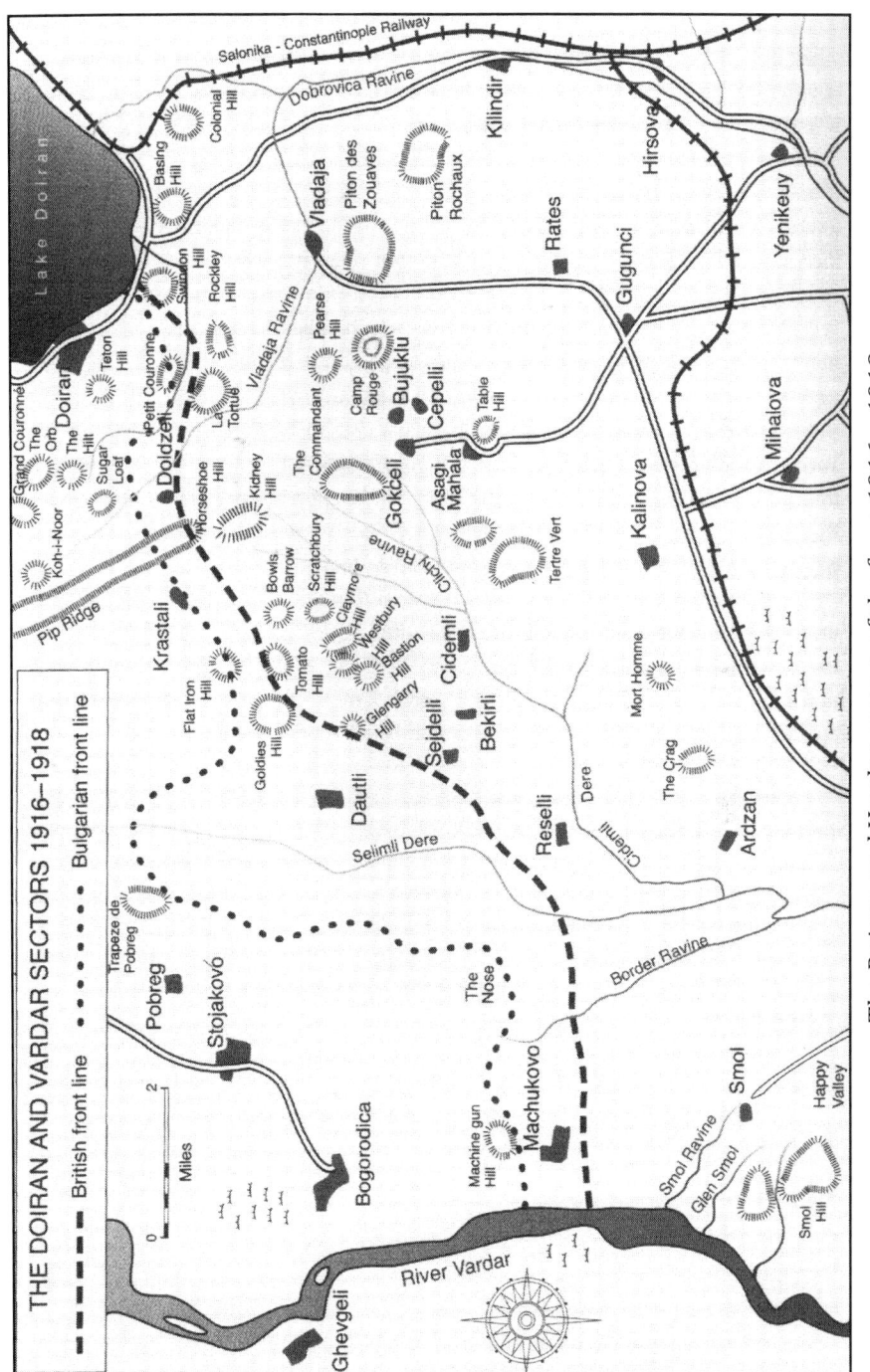

The Doiran and Vardar sectors of the front 1916 – 1918.

25 October 1917
The French are smashing away on our left[64]. They made an advance on the 23rd and have taken trenches from the Bulgars. Our boys made a sham attack to keep Johnny busy and away from the French. Johnny is putting plenty of shells over on the road and Tomato Hill and back of gun position, but did not find gun.

26 October 1917
Dugout had fallen in owing to the rain. Had to build it again and almost finished by Stand To.

27 October 1917
Went on sentry. It's a glorious night, full moon. Nice, quiet and bright.

28 October 1917
Ham came over in afternoon. Got orders to go digging at Bowl's Barrow to make emplacement. Worked 'til about 11:00 p.m. Went back to gun for rest of night.

29 October 1917
Went to Bowl's Barrow to put up barrage stops in new emplacement. Got back to camp before tea.

30 October 1917
Went to Whaleback to strip dugouts of reusable materials. Went back to gun in evening. Johnny sent over whizz bangs at back of hill while I was crossing. Made a dart for camp. He also sent some high explosive shells on the road and P 4 ½ and Tomato Hill. Quite busy (what...).

---

[64] The French advance referred to was taking place west of Lake Ochrid into Albania. Operations halted quickly due to Italian pressure as the latter did not want French forces getting involved in what the Italian government and military saw as their sphere of influence.

"Got orders to go digging at Bowl's Barrow to make emplacement. Worked 'til about 11:00 p.m.," 28 October 1918

31 October 1917
Old Charlie, my No.2, went sick. Johnny still going strong sending 'em over at back of camp. Too near to be comfortable. Rather quiet during the night.

1 November 1917
In afternoon at 5:00 p.m. five Taubes came over, expected a raid but they were driven off by our gunfire except one who kept over the Pips and had a game of his own by turning his machine gun on the boys

in the trenches. Where he was, our guns could not get to him owing to the hills as he kept rather low. The boys gave him a dose of his own stuff by turning their machine guns on him and drove him off. Mounted our guns for the night (quiet).

2 November 1917
Went with Ham to find emplacement before Stand Down this morning as I have to do some strafing. Found one on the slopes of Tomato Hill and have to renovate it this evening and drive stakes in for barraging. Fire on Flat Iron Hill at 10:00 a.m. this morning and guns strafed Johnny. He retaliated on some eighteen of our guns and the first shell found one near the road leading round the bottom of Scratchbury Hill going through the shield and exploding at the tail and turning the gun upside down and killing the team. Firing on Flat Iron Hill was a wash out for tonight.

3 November 1917
Boys still going at it with artillery. Some Taubes over, bombs dropped but no damage done. Whilst we were getting tea Johnny directed whizz-bangs on us in our camp to catch us on the hop but he was too late. We cleared off to safer quarters. Going to fire on Flat Iron Hill tonight. Got gun and ammunition ready, went up to Tomato Hill at 7:00 p.m. and fired 2000 rounds. Finished firing at 4:00 a.m. on the 4th.

4 November 1917
Went to sleep after breakfast. Cleaned gun and filled belts with fresh ammunition in afternoon. Johnny still sending his shells all over the place. Went to Claymore, our old emplacement at 9:00 p.m., South Lancashires sent up rocket from Bowl's Barrow for the R.F.A. to open up with a barrage and all along the line they sent it. At 11:00 p.m. the Black Watch went for The Nose and South Lancashires to Flat Iron. Raid was a success.[65]

---

[65] The two raids mentioned here were in fact diversions to draw Bulgarian attention away from an attack by the 12th Argyll and Sutherland Highlanders on Boyau Hill, half way between The Nose and Trapeze de Stojakovo. The 10th Black Watch sent two officers and 40 men to make a demonstration against

DIARY DURING MY PERIOD IN SALONIKA

5 November 1917
Had to go to headquarters to draw winter kit and get another man for my gun team to take the place of the one who went to hospital. Rather a quiet night.

6 November 1917
I had a rest all day as my men went on different jobs.

7 November 1917
Started a new dugout. Raining all day. Fired on Flat Iron Hill at night, 2000 rounds in total.

8 November 1917
Still raining. Johnny put some shells in camp. Not much damage.

9 November 1917
Raining all day. Our old dugout fell in. Moved into new one that was only half finished. Went up to gun position. Saw Johnny put a barrage

---

a defensive work 200 yards south east of the Pyramide and Trapeze de Stojakovo (a further party of an officer and 40 men acted as a flank guard for the main attack on Boyau Hill). The raiders were not to risk heavy casualties. Once the bombardment of Boyau Hill began, the Black Watch advanced and fired rifle grenades. The Bulgarians opened a heavy fire and the raiding party retired having sustained casualties of four men wounded. In addition, the flank protection party supplied by the Black Watch lost one man killed and three wounded. At the same time the 9th South Lancashires raided the village of Selimli. 'A' Company provided four officers and 120 men, 'B' Company one NCO, 20 men and a Lewis gun team and 'C' Company an officer, 20 men and a Lewis gun team. The village was rushed at 2335 hours. No enemy troops were located and after 45 minutes the raiders returned without suffering any casualties. Whilst these diversionary operations were in progress, three officers, 100 men from the 12th Argyll and Sutherland Highlanders, plus a party of Royal Engineers, attacked Boyau Hill. Entering the Bulgarian position the raiding party destroyed three machine guns before withdrawing with the casualties of three officers, 38 men and seven engineers wounded.

on the Pips as 8*th* King's Shropshire Light Infantry had given them a bombing raid⁶⁶.

10 November 1917
Relieved by 26*th* Division. Back at camp by 12:00 p.m.

11 November 1917
Cleaned mud from ourselves during morning. Church parade in afternoon and after that revolver shooting.

12 November 1917
Built dugout for stores.

13 November 1917
Rained all day and in went this dugout so shifted into yet another.

14 November 1917
Went with the C.O. to find reserve line emplacements. It's an amazing affair going out with him. He is deaf and every time a shell came over we had to pat him on the back so that he would get down. This time the C.O., a captain and myself were out to mark off emplacements; C.O. and Captain in front and myself behind with the markers. While walking along the screened path beside the 420 Road a 5.9 shell screamed toward us. I, of course, got down as did the captain who forgot about the old chap being deaf. To see the Commanding Officer walking along as though on a lane in England, taking not the slightest notice of bursting shells was a sight to see. Then he looked around and saw us about 200 yards behind, trying to bury ourselves in the earth. On seeing the smoke from the shells he guessed what was up and tried to bury himself. After that we completed our jobs and returned to camp.

---

[66] There is no reference to a raid by the 8*th* KSLI in their war diary. Instead, this could be a reference to a patrol on the night of 8-9 November by 21 men under 2*nd* Lieutenant Murphy, which laid up at the north end of Rhyl Ravine in anticipation of ambushing a Bulgarian patrol. The war diary records that no enemy troops were met.

16 November 1917
Went to trenches on Bagatelle. Still raining. Finished work on emplacement at about 11:00 a.m. Wet to the skin, mud all over us. We returned and got into dry clothes.

17 November 1917
Went to Bagatelle again for revetting trenches.

18 November 1917
Another day revetting.

19 November 1917
Finished work on Bagatelle at 3:00 p.m. in the afternoon and returned to camp. Found another job needed doing at Bagatelle - emplacement to make.

20 November 1917
Went to signals dugout to act as assistant signaler.[67] It's a good job. I do not know anything about it so they will teach me before I do much. We are also going to fix up a concert for Christmas. We commenced practicing today.

21 November 1917
Still with signals.

22 November 1917
At 9:30 p.m., Johnny attacked 26th Division just on our left. He got caught between his own barrage and ours which caused him heavy casualties. Our boys were carrying in his wounded well into the morning. He got pretty near to our wire. In cases like this we sort of call an armistice until all the wounded are brought in.[68]

---

[67] George is trained as signaler for the first time.
[68] This is a reference to an attack on Glengarry Hill at 2100 hours by 100 Bulgarians following an intensive 15 minute bombardment. Although the raiding force got onto the hill a defensive barrage of artillery, mortars and rifle grenades forced them back. At 2122 hours the British artillery barrage

23 November 1917
Rather quiet until the evening. About 10:30 p.m. Johnny had another go at us but he got another smashing.[69] *Our No.3 Section was just getting relieved by the 65th Brigade but were kept in the line owing to Johnny attacking. He sent plenty of shells and gas in Bujuklu Ravine and Pearse Ravine.*

24 November 1917
Quiet all day. While on duty 2 a.m. 'til 4 a.m. this morning (the 25th) Johnny attacked again.[70] *They are going very strong. Will know later how things went.*

25 November 1917
Johnny was repulsed early this morning. Our boys retaliated early this morning and gave him a hiding.

26 November 1917
Rather quiet except for a few shells over during the night.

27 November 1917
Another fine day. Quiet during night.

---

    was lengthened to catch Bulgarian troops retiring across no-man's-land. During the attack only a single British soldier was wounded. No information is given in the 26th Division summary as to Bulgarian casualties.

[69] Here, George is mentioning an attack by a large group of Bulgarians on P4 ½, held as part of 22nd Division's front. The attacking force reached but could not penetrate the British wire and lost at least 16 men killed and two taken prisoner.

[70] George is mistaken here in thinking the Bulgarians had attacked again. Instead, as a 26th Division Summary for the 24 hours ending 6 a.m. on 25 November 1917 states, British artillery opened heavy fire between 0310 – 0420 hours on 25 November. The guns concentrated on established barrage lines and blocking points in case the Bulgarians launched an attack. The reason for this activity was a previous heavy Bulgarian bombardment of K and L Sectors, which appeared to herald an attack.

28 November 1917
A Taube over and dropped some bombs and returned again at 10:30 p.m., bombed Janes. Day fine.

29 November 1917
Taubes over again and more bombs dropped. Day fine.

30 November 1917
Got paid, so that made another fine day. Getting very cold.

31 November 1917
Easy today, but very windy. Went to Expeditionary Force Canteen to spend some of our pay.

1 December 1917
It's a dull life out of the trenches. Just inspection and nothing else. [71]
Went to Clickity Clicks (66th Brigade) Concert Party. Not so bad.

2 December 1917
Had a proper concert of our own. Got stage fixed up. Went as a girl (some girl). Still had a jolly evening.

3 December 1917
It is getting very cold at night, it blew awful. Our dugout had tin sheet torn on the roof and every moment I expected it to be lifted off. The

---

[71] Despite George comments on little activity and boredom leading up to Christmas 1917, the 66th MGC War Diary records for the period: "A great deal of training has been done during the 1st three weeks of this period. All ranks of the MG classification practiced a revolver course. Gas and bombing officers were appointed and gave good instruction. Officers received training in their duties as to the case of arrivals, packsaddling. A daily parade in close order was held which included physical training, for smartening up purposes. A cup was given for an intersectional competition which included all branches of training and such games as Football, Hockey, Cricket, Tug of War, etc. There were also mounted and dismounted sports, which was very successful."

wind appeared to come from all quarters and the fire went out owing to lack of fuel. It was like being in a cold storage.

4 December 1917
Mess orderly today. Saw Clickity Clicks in evening. Still very cold. Done duty from 10:00 p.m. 'til 2:00 a.m. Fire in dugout so not so cold.

5 December 1917
Went to Expeditionary Force Canteen. Spent 15 Drakma and bought plenty of cigs.

6 December 1917
Fed up with cold and nothing to do.

7 December 1917
Weather at freezing point. Brrrrrr.

8 December 1917
If things don't liven up will have nothing to write about. Went to E.F. Canteen with Staples.

9 December 1917
Wind dropped. Staples and myself went to E.F. Canteen again and on our way saw three large wild mountain dogs. Awful brutes! They were after a mule so we made a circuit round them as we did not have anything to protect ourselves in case they took a liking to us. So said that if we came tomorrow we would take our revolvers. They were still there when we returned.

10 December 1917
Staples and I went to E.F. Canteen again, this time we put 3 rounds in our revolver in case of accidents. Got near the dogs but when we got our revolvers out they bolted. There was no way of creeping up on the dogs as the place was so open, which was lucky for them. Spent the last of our pay at the canteen and so back to camp.

DIARY DURING MY PERIOD IN SALONIKA

11 December 1917
Rained all day. We stayed in dugout and played cards.

12 December 1917
Went to the baths in morning and had rum issue in evening. Staples had too much and gave us an evening entertainment.

13 December 1917
Another dismal day. I think I shall finish writing for a while, it's really not worth it. It is getting too dull.

17 December 1917
Joy! The Christmas Parcel has come. Books, cake etc. We will have a time of it.

19 December 1917
Things are going strong up the line.

24 December 1917
Every day up to today we have had a practice for concert and everything is alright. In one skit I have to be a cowboy, all complete from hat to spurs. We have borrowed marquees and tables from the stores at Gugunci for our homemade concert party.

25 December 1917
Christmas Day. It is a nice day. Fixed up stage in a double marquee after dinner, which was at 5:00 p.m. Wonders of wonders....it was real Christmassy. Turkeys, beef, potato, pudding, custard, beer, mineral water, nuts, oranges, etc. and plenty of figs. Goodness knows where they got 'em from, but it was the best dinner we had for three years. Everyone was happy. Our show started at 6:30 p.m. and over at 9:30 p.m. and was quite a success. Had what we wanted after it was over. It is 1:30 a.m. on the 26th, but I hope that next Christmas will be spent at home.[72]

---

[72] 66th MGC War Diary for Christmas 1917: The usual festivities were held during Xmas week and the men were well-catered for by the canteen. 1000 francs were spent from the canteen funds for their Xmas dinners. There

"In a skit, I have to be a cowboy, all complete from hat to spurs,"
24 December 1917

---

was a very successful concert on Xmas night, well organized and carried out by Deas and Wood. A large number of officers and NCOs and a few selected men were able to take 3 days leave in the town of Salonika. This privilege was much appreciated by the NCOs and men, since they had been in or near the line for over a year with the exception of a short time away during the spring of 1917.

DIARY DURING MY PERIOD IN SALONIKA

26 December 1917
Prepared to go up the line. Bill and I started on our own. Raining and cold. The roads were about a foot deep in mud, so we just splashed through it singing to our hearts content. Arrived at new quarters covered in mud. New quarters at Wiltshire Ravine near Doiran.

27 December 1917[73]
Another dismal day.

28 December 1917
Still raining. Johnny still shelling our camp. Not so monotonous.

29 December 1917
Laid telephone line from transport to headquarters. Transport about 2 miles back at Box Hill. Took our revolvers with us in case there may be something to shoot, but all we saw was a golden eagle. Beautiful birds. Would like to have shot him, almost did, but was rather glad that I missed him. To see them flying and gliding about is a sight to see. And the name golden fits well. They are golden.

30 December 1917[74]
At 6:30 p.m. our boys opened out with big guns and so did Johnny. Things not so dull!

---

[73] 66th MGC War Diary, 27 – 29 December 1917: Several officers rejoined the company from hospital. The company relieved the 67th MGC in the right subsector without incident. A conference was held at Brigade HQ for commanding officers at which the work to be done by the company was detailed. There was a very large amount to be done, mainly owing to the decision to group guns more closely together for better control and barrage fire. The guns taken over were employed singly at large distances apart which made the control of more than one gun in action, an impossibility for a section commander.

[74] 66th MGC War Diary 30 December 1917: 24 men were attached from the infantry to be trained in reserve as machine gunners in the event of casualties on the same day. The details of the new proposal Part I (instructional) MG course together with the necessary target success, was received for remarks from Divisional HQ and it was decided that the men under instruction should

31 December 1917
Being New Year's Night we waited until midnight. The boys opened out and gave Johnny some good wishes. One remarkable point was from Johnny's trenches came the sound of Rule Britannia being played on their band just before 12:00 a.m. So we gave them a good idea that we were still ruling and that shut him up.

1 January 1918
Why people get so drunk I cannot make out. During the night the other four signallers were helpless and I had to stick and do the duty all night until breakfast. When I was relieved I just rolled over and went to sleep.

2 January 1918
Some gas over so we had to wear our helmets for a while, uncomfortable things.

3 January 1918
Very quiet.

4 January 1918
Taken off signals to go up the line. Not sorry to be back with boys and the old gun again.

5 January 1918
Went up to Shropshire Ravine, joined Section at 8:30 a.m. In the afternoon, McDonald and myself took Read to Field Ambulance as he was sick. Coming back or rather just before we left I said "So long Read, I'll be down with you soon." Not dreaming, how true my words were. Then we left him. On our way back I felt a tickly feeling down

---

fire the course, after they had received sufficient preliminary instruction. The Company was kept up to strength by reinforcements during the month.
An inspector of ordinance carried out an inspection of the men of the company and condemned several tripods from which there had been an excess amount of firing. He also made it possible for the company to obtain several spare parts which they have never been issued with.

my spine and I said to McDonald. "Mac, what's wrong, I feel windy." "Rot," old Mac said. "Well there is something wrong that I cannot understand. I have never felt like this before." "Oh", he said. "You will soon be alright." But no, I'll admit, I did feel windy. But on getting back to camp, I felt myself again. After tea, I got orders to go to Tortoise Hill in the morning to build gun dugout and take with me Gaunt and Williams. After that I got to bed.

6 January 1918
At 8:30 a.m. the three of us went to Tortoise. Our way led though Rockley, up Tortoise Ravine, through communications trench and over hill on top to trenches. Found the spot we have to go to on top of trench.

To get to dugout we had to crawl through narrow slit so that Johnny could not see us and we had to dig under wire netting in case aircraft came over. We worked until about 12:00 p.m. and then had some lunch. We were disturbed twice by planes but luckily were not seen. At 2:30 p.m., Johnny opened out and it became too uncomfortable on top so we cleared out into a trench forgetting our kit and gas helmets. We made for a dugout about twelve yards away and when inside discovered that there was no blanket covering to keep out gas and also that we had left our gas helmets behind. He was sending over gas so we made a dash back for our helmets. Gaunt said "I'll get up and tie the kit together and you two drag it through the cutting. " I argued that it was two narrow. But off went Gaunt. It seemed hours his tying the kits together and then we pulled, but they stuck. Damn it! William and I dropped the string, scrambled over the top got our kit and scrambled back into dugout. Johnny eased up, so we proceeded out of the trench, got to ravine and saw his shells pounding away at the bottom. We stayed at the top for awhile. He finished and altered range to Rockley, so we came down, passed through camp where the cookhouse had just been hit, the poor cook was almost crying with rage. Got halfway between ravine and Rockley when he pounded both places at once.

"He was sending over gas, so we made a dash back for our helmets,"
6 January 1918

We quickly lay on the ground sweating and hoping his fire would not hit the path. We did feel uncomfortable. At last he stopped so we ran the final 500 yards to Rockley. Got into a bombproof dugout and was offered some tea, then went on back to camp at 5:00 p.m. Just after arriving shelling started - 'Bang'! shrapnel burst so we quickly got into the nearest dugout. About three minutes after - 'Biff.' Another heavy shrapnel shell - so we got further into the dugout. Then 'Crack'! - I got it right in the leg near my groin. If my head had been more forward I would have had it in the head as I was sitting down. William helped me to the Dressing Station. That night I was laid on a stretcher that was suspended between two large wheels and attached to the stretcher were two shafts so that a mule could be placed between them for traction. Well, you can imagine going up an incline one was if not holding the sides of the stretcher to start to slide off feet first and on going down one would slide the other way the head almost going between the mules rear legs. Well you can imagine my plight that mule excreting wind from the time he started to pull my stretcher

DIARY DURING MY PERIOD IN SALONIKA

until I got to the 66th Field Ambulance Casualty Clearing Station.[75] Here my wound was inspected by a Medical Officer and the shrapnel ball was found to be dangerously near a main artery.

7 January 1918
Went to 31st Casualty Clearing Station. Operation on leg as soon as I arrived. Ball extracted, which orderly gave me as souvenir. I'm going to have a rest from the front line so somehow the wound seems worth it.

8 January 1918
Still in 31st C.C.S at Janes.

9 January 1918[76]
Sent to 28th General Hospital in Salonika.

---

[75] A Casualty Clearing Station was part of the casualty evacuation chain, further back from the front line than Aid Posts and Field Ambulances. It was manned by troops of the Royal Army Medical Corps, with men from the Royal Army Service Corps and Royal Engineers attached. The job of a CCS was to treat casualties sufficiently to allow their return to duty or enable the more seriously wounded to be evacuated to base hospitals. The CCS was not a place for casualties to have a long-term stay. To enable easy transfer of casualties to base hospitals, a CCS was usually located on or near railway lines or main roads. Although quite large, a CCS was a fully mobile unit.

[76] Whilst George was away from the Company in January the unit War Diary states that the whole Company worked on bombproof emplacements, dugouts and splinter-proof emplacements. No operations of any importance were carried out on the unit's front, although 2 guns cooperated with 65th Brigade on the morning of 25 January 1918. Bulgarian artillery, trench mortars and machine guns were active and the Company replied to this fire each night. Several large drafts arrived to boost numbers in the Company. These were mostly men who had previously gone to hospital. On 3 January, Major C.C. Tee left the Company to become Divisional Machine Gun Officer for 22nd Division. Between 3 and 25 January the Company was commanded by Lieutenant Campbell. On the latter date Captain Holmes-Jackson assumed temporary command of the Company with Lieutenant P B Deas as second-in-command. The 2 officers from the Company were attached to the R.F.A. for a course of instruction on barrages.

21 January 1918
After a good time in hospital I had to have another operation on my leg and nearly snuffed it. The sister said I had too much gas and the way they said they hit me about to bring me round was something to think about.

12 February 1918[77]
Discharged from hospital.

14 February 1918
Went to No.5 Convalescent Camp and am having electric treatment and massage[78].

17 February 1918
Sunday, it has been snowing for twenty-four hours and it drifted to five feet deep in camp. To get to mess rooms we had to cut pathways. In the open fields it was eighteen inches deep. It is still coming down. After every meal we all get between the blankets.

---

[77] With George still suffering from his wound, 66th MGC remained in the line at Doiran. The Company War Diary for February 1918 records that the new tactical grouping of machine guns was working well, although four days of poor weather including snow had caused delays. No operations of note took place during the month. However, the Company's guns fired around 230,000 rounds on various targets such as tracks, roads and working parties with good results. Much work was done by section commanders to making new barrage maps and grids. A refresher course for Machine Gun Officers was held at the HQ of the Reserve Company under the Divisional Machine Gun Officer and was attended by four officers from the Company.

[78] Electrotherapy was part of orthopaedic treatment available to the wounded during the First World War. It was used in the examination of nerve injuries to establish the extent of nerve damage. Electrical stimulation was also used on paralysed muscles that had been sutured and were healing and regenerating.

DIARY DURING MY PERIOD IN SALONIKA

22 February 1918
Went to concert and had to stand up all the time which caused a boil on the wound. Wondered what was wrong. Reported sick and doctor ordered poultices to be put on my leg to draw the puss.

1 March 1918
Whilst having wound dressed this morning a piece of India rubber glove came out of wound. When sewing it up they snipped a piece off glove and left it in.

6 March 1918
Leg still bad, had to get to bed.

10 March 1918
Went to see footer match between French and our boys. We won 5-1.

13 March 1918[79]
At 8:00 a.m. this morning I came over feeling really bad. Had a swelling as big as a football at the back of my leg and my orderly got the wind up and rushed for doctor. Temperature went up to 102. Doctor immediately sent me to hospital.

14 March 1918
This morning went under operation. Had leg opened up and piece of leather jerkin was taken out. I'd been wearing that when wounded. The ball had carried the piece into the wound and it was not removed when the ball was taken out. If it had not been taken out then (today),

---

[79] With George about to undergo further surgery, his comrades in 66th MGC were relieved in the front line at the beginning of March by 65th MGC. The Company went into divisional reserve at Three Trees Fountain. Here they spent most of the month training. During this time, Lieutenant E.C. Hudson arrived and assumed command. On 27 March a draft of 11 men arrived as replacements for sick men being evacuated to the UK under the "Y" Scheme.

I might have lost leg, so the doctor said. I could hardly sleep thinking about it.[80]

2 May 1918
Discharged from hospital.[81]

3 May 1918
Was expected to march to camp with full pack, but leg would not carry me. Was put back in ward.

5 May 1918
Still expected to march to camp but I'm blessed if I will. I've had enough trouble with my leg as it is.

7 May 1918
Major came round. "Any complaint?" he said. I told him I could not march to camp with full pack. He said I could. I said I cannot. He disagreed. The best of it is it is my leg, not his. He cannot feel the pain. So I asked to see the commanding officer.

---

[80] Following his operation in March, George continued his recuperation during April. During this month his fellow machine gunners were back in the line at Doiran. Each night the Company's Vickers guns carried out harassing fire on Bulgarian camps and tracks. Between 18 and 22 April the Company was involved in laying down a heavy bombardment, firing some 150,000 rounds. After such concentrated firing many of the guns showed considerable signs of wear. The Bulgarians retaliated with their own machine gun fire. On 29 April 30 men from the infantry were attached to the Company and trained in gunnery to bring the unit's strength up to where each gun had a 6 man team.

[81] Although George was discharged from hospital on 2 May, it would still be over a month before he rejoined his unit. During his continued absence 66th MGC continued to be busy laying down regular harassing fire on key positions in the Bulgarian lines including P4, Emerald Hill, Krastali village and the Volovec track. Throughout the month, two of the Company's Vickers guns were tasked with each firing 4,000 rounds onto selected points behind Petit Couronné. Other guns were posted at positions west of Pip Ridge to cover parts of the British front line.

DIARY DURING MY PERIOD IN SALONIKA

8 May 1918
Saw commanding officer. He asked if I could manage to walk in my own time with somebody to carry my kit. I said I would as not having the pack would make a lot of difference. Went to No.2 Camp and the C.O. of the hospital sent him a note about me.

C.O.: "Um, you're Burford?"
Me: "Yes, Sir."
C.O.: "Let me see you walk. Now look boy, there is no need for you to swing your leg like that."
Me: "But I cannot help it."
C.O: "Now try and walk properly. Do it, ready, that's right. Have another go. No, there's no need to limp. Let's have a look your leg." I showed him.
C.O.: "Hey, Sergeant Major, send this man to No.5 Convalescent Camp". Relief, I thought he was going to say (undecipherable)! "He ought not to have been sent here at all."
Left No.2 at 3:00 p.m. and here I am.

30 May 1918
Discharged from Convalescent Camp and sent to Summer Hill Camp at Salonika.

5 June 1918[82]
Sent up the line, put on signals, as my leg was not fit for standing in trench.

---

[82] 66th MGC War Diary, 1 – 30 June 1918: The Company was relieved by the 65 MGC on the left subsection on the nights of 2/3 and 3/4. The relief was carried out without incident. The Company proceeded to THREE TREES FOUNTAIN in Divisional Reserve. Various forms of training have been carried out including the following: Gas Drill, Firing in Gasmasks on the Range, Revolver Shooting, General instruction of attached men and doubtful gunners, squad drill. The training was interrupted from 13-19 June owing to all available men being employed on consolidation work in the Divisional area for anti-malarial purposes.
Various competitions…have taken place for the Major General's Cup. The latter acted as judge in this turnout competition and expressed his satisfaction at the general cleanliness and smartness of all ranks on parade.

20 June 1918
Went to transport signals section. Johnny opened out with a barrage on line and reserves.

21 June 1918
Johnny gave us another display.

22 June 1918
Another bombardment today.

23 June 1918
Another. It's rather dull on transport. Every time I take messages to Corporal Heyward he is either at headquarters or asleep in his tent. Still, I rather like him and he is a good fellow. Never worries us much and he don't like messages because they are nothing but getting us to run about for the officers' pleasure and I sympathize with him.

27 June 1918
Telephone wire broke, evidently hit by shell, I'm ordered to go out and repair it. Walked about ½ mile before finding the break, repaired wire and sat down for a smoke before returning to dugout. Just then a Taube came flying overhead scouting behind our lines. Then, out of the clouds suddenly shot one of our aeroplanes and engaged him in a scrap and what a scrap. Up and down they went, round and round. Each trying to send a burst of machine gun fire into the other. I thought at first the Taube seemed to get the better of it until he suddenly went shooting over his lines with our plane after him. As they went across the lines the Taube seemed to drop. Just after that

---

At the Divisional Horse Show the Company won the turnout competition versus 65 and 67 MGC Companies.

The Company is to have the new establishment of 20 guns, etc. as per GS (SD) 269. Lieutenant P.B. Deas has been in command of the Company from 13th to present date during the absence of Captain E. C. Hudson on duty on the retired line with Colonel Barnard, MGC 16th Corps. The general health of the company improved toward the end of the month and there is now little sickness.

DIARY DURING MY PERIOD IN SALONIKA

one of our bombing squadrons appeared. I expect that lone aeroplane of ours was out scouting for the bombers when he saw and tackled the Taube. The bombers kept right on towards the enemy lines. I expect they had plenty of eggs for him.

16 July 1918
When things are dull, I have not bothered about writing. Today our boys are getting an extra supply of ammunition for barraging.

24 July 1918[83]
It is the 24th and we have to be smashing away at the Bulgar. He is doing the same to us. Our boys expected to go over on the 28th as the French and Greeks are going to advance. Johnny put an extra barrage up on the 23rd and 24th and came over on the night of the 24th and 25th on Hill 380 and took back with him some machine guns. One in the eye for us.

26 July 1918
Quiet except for our planes. They have been bombing the Bulgars every day.

27 July 1918
Today is the 27th. Out of bed at 7:00 a.m. It is meant to be my morning off duty. But, because of that the wire broke, so I went out and repaired it. Fritz sent a plane over to bring down one of our balloons, but one of our planes stopped him. It was a great fight. First ours on

---

[83] 66th MGC War Diary, 19 – 20 July 1918: "The enemy was expected to relieve the "O" trenches (0.1, 0.2, 0.3, and perhaps 0.4). Machine guns fired with the artillery on all tracks, etc. which the enemy might use…Guns fired well, but some showed considerable wear after the firing. Barrels did not last long… fired 115,000 rounds.

24 July 1918: On the night of 24/25, the enemy attempted to raid AB4 (in front of ROCKLEY) SP1 and MAMELON. The two latter had been expected for some days. All 16 guns in the line fired within barrage times in response to light signals during the night. In no part of the brigade front could the raids be considered successful. (George's statement of the loss of some machine guns is in conflict with this diary entry).

top, then Fritz, then round and round each other. Then suddenly Fritz shied off, ours followed him over his own line and brought him down. At the same time, one of our bombing squadrons returned, ten of 'em. It's a sight to see a couple of planes scrapping and better to see Jerry sent to earth.

28 July 1918
Quiet all day except in the evening. Johnny sent over a barrage and again at 10:00 p.m. Our boys not going over after all.

29 July 1918
Another quiet day.

30 July 1918
Quiet during day until just after "Stand To". The Shropshires and Lancashire Regiment made a raid on Johnny.[84] The guns are kicking up a row. At a quarter past 10:00 p.m., the boys had another go at him and the French have been hitting him since 10:00 p.m. Expect they are going over. It is 11:00 p.m. and they are all still going strong. But I am going to sleep. Goodnight.

31 July 1918
Very quiet.

1 August 1918
Same.

2 August 1918
It is blisteringly hot and I had to go out and repair wire and found that there had been a grassfire which had burnt about 60 yards of it.

---

[84] This appears to be a reference to a raid made by 1 sergeant and 8 men of the 8th KSLI on 28 July against Bulgarian positions at O6. The raiding party entered the enemy trenches at 23.30 hours and killed two Bulgarian soldiers before being forced to retire. The raiders suffered no casualties. The war diaries of the 8th KSLI and 9th South Lancashires (both in 66th Brigade) do not record any activity on 30 July.

A nice job laying wire in the scorching sun, but I just joined it together and laid fresh wire in the evening while cool. At night the French went for Johnny again. Our boys had a rest, only sending a few over.

3 August 1918
It was very hot today, too hot to move, so just laid down and said bad things against the heat. Some Taubes over.

4 August 1918
Busy day today. We got some whitewash and done the dugout. Whitewash flying all over the place. Some fellows who came up for a talk soon went running out. The splashing of white wash was too much for them. We got everything we could out of the dugout. After plenty of laughs and fun and splashing about, Lieutenant Eccles came in unexpected and got a brush full of whitewash. His face was a picture and the language – tut tut! Once the whitewashing was finished we put up a couple of shelves for photos and stuck pictures on the walls. It looked a perfect picture, so did we covered head to toe in whitewash! During the night the French and our boys were at it again.

5 August 1918
Quiet day except at night.

6 August 1918
Same but a little bit too hot. The boys at it again. They say in Blighty we never do anything in Salonika. Well, they are right as it is only the Base. The same as Le Harve in France. But go up the line in Serbia, 60 miles from Salonika and see: still that does not matter. At 7:00 p.m. our boys opened up and let it rip. It was great. Johnny also had a cut, but we beat him. Our boys finished at 11:00 p.m., at least, as far as I know. I was asleep about 11:00 p.m.

7 August 1918
Nothing doing so far, just a bit of firing at 7:00 a.m.

"I could hardly find the wire...Up hill, down vale and through bushes on a very dark night, to find a break," 8 August 1918

8 August 1918
Bit busy today. Went out to repair wire and then it broke again at night about 9:30 p.m. So, had to go out and mend it again. While out our boys put two successive bombardments up, so did Johnny. The

flash of guns almost blinded me. I could hardly find the wire. It is not an easy job, uphill, down vale and through bushes on a very dark night, to find a break.

9 August 1918
I blessed if the wire did not break again. Found the break within 100 yards of headquarters on a hill where the Bulgar sends his shells near one of our batteries. Repaired it and got back as quickly as possible. Headquarters signals could have repaired it but they won't risk much.

10 August 1918
Wire gone again as we thought. Followed wire to headquarters, it was not broken but headquarters had us plugged out, so told them what I thought of them and that in future when wire broke we should both go half way. Corporal Thompson did not like it. He is alright miles away from the shells, but near them he is very windy and suffers from extra cold feet. The blighter has hardly ever been in the line, well only once and he got out of that as soon as possible. I'll admit, none of us are fond of shells, but there is a limit to everything. If Tommies cannot work half & half and help each other then it's not worth a candle.

11 August 1918
Quiet until 5:00 p.m. when Johnny shelled battery on side of hill that we occupy and they came a bit too close. At least they stopped sending heavies over even if they kept it up with shrapnel until 9:00 p.m.

12 August 1918
Quiet.

13 August 1918
Not much to do.

14 August 1918
An easy day.

15 August 1918
Went out on wire as far as Headquarters. Johnny started shelling battery. As I was in the vicinity, I cleared off.

16 August 1918
It is rumored that the Division is going out for training.

17 August 1918[85]
Sections in line are coming out. All equipment packed and ready to move off tomorrow.

18 August 1918
Reveille at 3:30 a.m., breakfast 4:30 a.m., at 8:30 a.m. loaded up equipment and joined headquarters at 9:30 a.m. Company then moved off. My leg not being fit for long trek I rode on the cook's wagon. Reached Kalabak at midnight.

21 August 1918
65th, 66th and 67th Machine Gun Companies are together.

22 August 1918
Wind very strong, tents were blown down. Bill and I tried to fix one up on our own. It was a struggle. Got it at last with the pole at about 90 degrees. Don't think it will last long until someone gives us a hand to make it stay.

23 August 1918
Nothing doing. [86]

---

[85] 66th MGC War Diary, 16 – 18 August 1918: On the night of 16/17 and 17/18 the company was relieved by the 83rd MGC and removed to training camp at HAJDARLI via THREE TREES.

[86] Although George records the remainder of August as a quiet time the 66th MGC War Diary for 21 to 31 August 1918 states that the Company spent much time training for offensive operations in open warfare. George's quiet time is probably due to his being with the signals section rather than back with his gun team.

DIARY DURING MY PERIOD IN SALONIKA

24 August 1918
Reported sick with leg, got excused P.T. That makes the third time I have had to report sick. Wish I was fit, so that I could get with pals in the company.

25 August 1918
Sunday, nothing to do. Was going to find a swimming pool, but left it.

26 August 1918
Went to find pool, walked about three miles, but it was worth it.

27 August 1918
Went again, but was not allowed in during heat of the day.

28 August 1918
Commanding Officer got an idea for swimming. Had a lorry to take us to Lake Ardzan about twelve miles away. It was great and the outing enjoyable.

30 August 1918
It was the turn of a party from the 67th Company to go to the lake so I thought I would like to go again. Went to get on lorry when an officer asked me what company I belonged to. "67th Sir." "Right, get up". Good job I am 'pally' with a lot of 67th, so they kept mum. So off I went again, to the envy of pals from my own company.

31 August 1918
Off to the lake again.

1 September 1918
Nothing doing. [87]

---

[87] Carrying on from August, the machine gun teams of George's unit continue training under direction of the Divisional Machine Gun Officer, whilst the signalers appear to have a much easier time.

2 September 1918
Same.

3 September 1918
Another swim in Lake Ardzan. I seem to be getting a cold.

4 September 1918
Had a sand and thunderstorm which ripped up the tents and a Bulgar observation balloon was blown over our lines and went off toward Salonika with an aeroplane after it. During the second and third day of this month our boys took some of Johnny's trenches and are still doing good work.[88] *But his defenses are a marvel, really impregnable but we will get him off the hills soon. We have our work cut out. It's not like fighting on the flat as it is all ravines and hills.*

5 September 1918
Rather an easy day of it.

6 September 1918
Expecting to move up the line.

---

[88] George is probably referring to the capture of the Roche Noire Salient by 2nd Gloucesters and 10th Hampshires of 82nd Brigade on 1 September 1918. The two battalions undertook 10 days training prior to the attack, including practice assaults over a full-size mock up of the position. A scale sand model was also used to instruct the troops. The Salient was located well in front of the main Bulgarian line and not directly connected by communication trenches. Wire cutting by artillery was undertaken between 25-27 August and on subsequent days artillery and machine gun barrages took place to keep open the gaps in the wire. The attack went in soon after 1730 hours on 1 September, the infantry quickly crossing the 300 yards of no-man's-land. Within an hour the two battalions had secured the position but came under heavy Bulgarian artillery fire. At 0500 hours on 2 September the Bulgarians launched a counter attack following a 30 minute bombardment. This assault was beaten off despite the Bulgarians gaining a foothold in the position. The operation cost the Gloucesters and Hampshires a total of 298 casualties. Bulgarian casualties are not recorded but they lost 67 men as prisoners.

7 September 1918
Stood by for moving off. Packed up and moved over the other side of the hill as we were to be isolated as Section is thought to have the flu.[89]

8 September 1918
It is the flu. All the companies have it[90].

9 September 1918
Only allowed 100 yards from camp so can't get the chance of a wash. At 6:00 p.m. we all had to take biscuit tins and water buckets and march to the water and wash there. Had then to bring back water for morning wash. It will always be the same until the flu is over.

10 September 1918
Up early this morning. Saw beautiful bombardment, it was like a panorama with the bursting and rumbling of shrapnel. We were out training for a big stunt but the "flu" has knocked it on the head up to now. In the evening we went to wash. I assure you it is a game getting all the tins and buckets together to fill with water. We're the laughing stock of other camps, but they also start their own isolation. Confound the "flu"!

13 September 1918
67th and 65th MG Companies are off up the line as only a few of them are down with the flu. There are 83 of our boys down with flu out of 140 so we are not much use. At 6:00 p.m. Bill Baldy and myself saddled up horses and laid wire to Kirec village. Not much of the village left. It is all smashed up. It was about 4 miles away. By the

---

[89] No mention of the flu in the unit diary.
[90] In early September 1918 an outbreak of influenza hit the 65th Brigade of 22nd Division. This proved so severe that by 7 September the decision was taken to withdraw the formation from the assault force preparing for the Second Battle of Doiran. 65th Brigade was placed in Army Reserve at Kirec and its place in the line was taken by 77th Brigade from 26th Division.

TAKE ME BACK TO BLIGHTY

DIARY DURING MY PERIOD IN SALONIKA

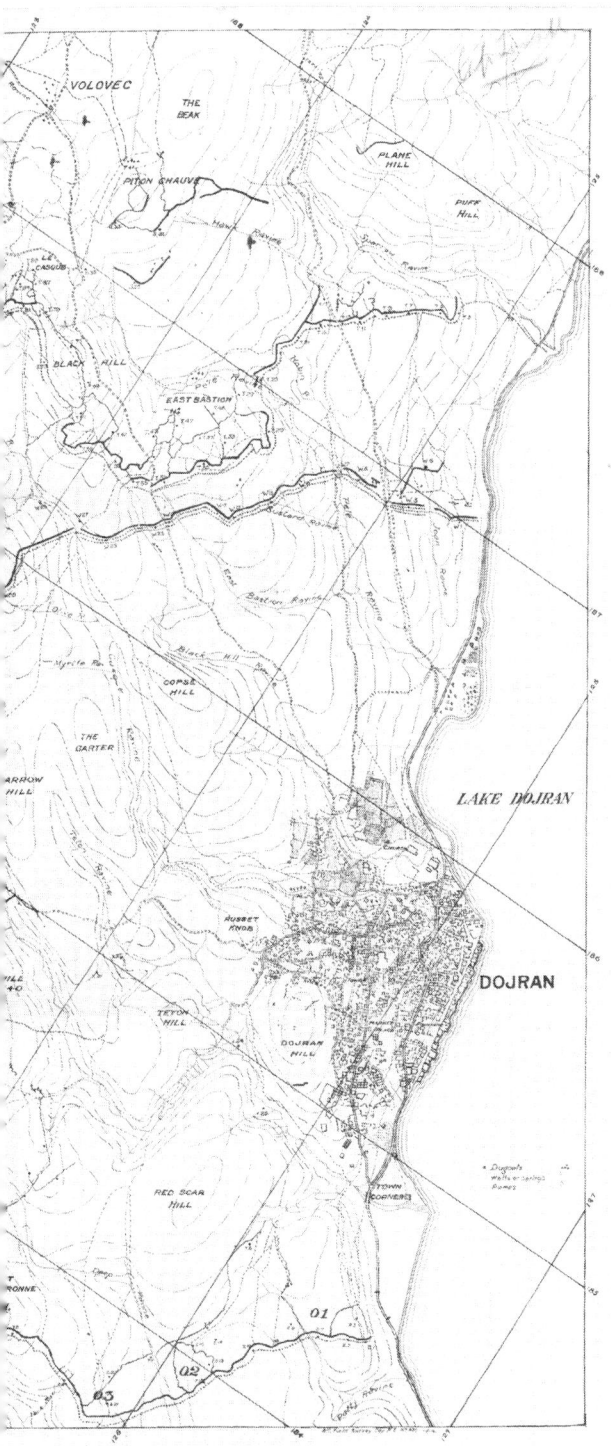

1:10,000 British trench map sheet Couronné marked up to show the frontage attacked by 22nd Division during the Second Battle of Doiran on 18 September 1918.

time we finished it was 9:00 p.m. so we went to the R.A.F. canteen[91]*. Back at camp about 11:00 p.m. Gave feed to horses and then into bed.*

14 September 1918
Wire broken on road. Took pick and dug a trench across the road. Put in wire and covered it. It won't get broken now. Easy day after that.

15 September 1918
Sunday. Nothing to do. At 4:00 p.m. this afternoon our artillery boys opened out for the stunt. Jove! Didn't it rip; they kept it up all night.[92]

16 September 1918
Rather quiet during the day. Heard the French made an advance on our left, plenty of prisoners and supplies being taken.[93] *Went out this afternoon to take message about three miles away. That's the good thing being a signaller, you can get out during the flu. At 6:30 p.m. the guns opened up. The stunt has commenced with a vengeance. It*

---

[91] A forward airfield had been established by No.47 Squadron (RFC) earlier in the campaign.

[92] This was the opening of the preliminary bombardment for the 2nd Battle of Doiran. For the battle, General Milne gathered 231 guns, including 36 x 60-pounders, 36 x 6-inch guns, 3 x 6-inch guns and 4 x 8-inch howitzers. This force was put together by stripping out most of the artillery from 26th and 27th Divisions west of Pip Ridge. Despite two days of successful wire cutting this artillery force would prove insufficient for the task. Milne attempted to improve the striking power of his artillery through the use of gas shells. Unfortunately, the demands of the Western Front ensured only a limited supply of chemical shells was sent to Salonika and when these were employed the gas tended to disperse quickly on the hills even in light wind.

[93] The main Allied offensive began on 15 September 1918 with the Battle of Dobropolje, an attack on three significant mountain peaks in the Moglena range by the six divisions of the Serbian 1st and 2nd Armies supported by two French divisions. The offensive aimed to take the villages of Gradsko and Krivolak, which were at the heart of German and Bulgarian road and rail communications. By late afternoon on 17 September the Franco-Serbian forces had pushed through the mountains. The following day, as Milne's forces attacked at Doiran, German and Bulgarian commanders held a crisis meeting in Prelip.

is neck or nothing now. If it was not for the hills, confound them, we would have had the Bulgar and the rest of 'em long ago. The crash of the bombardment is terrific and non-stop. We have got to get him off the hills this time, but it is going to be a job.

17 September 1918
Although we are as yet not in the line it's great to hear the shells ripping over to Johnny and the 'hum-hum' as they rush along through the air and the 'crash-crump' as the big 'uns burst on the hills and in the ravines intermixed with the burst of shrapnel. Also, the 'tut-tut-tut' of the machine guns. More guns joined in the song and medley at 11:00 p.m. and after four hours more of smashing at Johnny the boys went over.

18 September 1918[94]
At 3:00 p.m. today the boys got to Hill 535 and Johnny is bombarding for a counterattack. It is now 9:00 p.m. and I am sitting writing this as the news comes through. Sadly, by 9:30 p.m. the boys were driven back almost to their old position. The 77th Brigade are ready to go over any minute. Poor chaps, good luck to 'em, we have heard nothing of the 67th Brigade or the Greeks. The old man is in and out of the tent tearing his hair and asking for news but there is little to give him. Let's hope we get some better news through. There are aeroplanes up galore and these have been bombing Johnny. Backwards and forward they go each time returning empty, filling up and the returning to take the fight to Johnny. The rumbling of the barrage is beyond description. A few of the busy ladies of England want to just have a peek at it and that will alter their cry: "What are the boys doing in Salonika?" An air raid would be enough for them. There is plenty of excitement in the air. 'Baldy' just received a message for the C.O. to get ready for moving up any minute, even though the flu has cut our company to half strength. Hurrah! Another message that our boys are getting on

---

[94] 66th MGC War Diary, 18 September 1918: Orders received at 12:45 that the Company was to move to TABLE in lorries. At 1300 hrs TABLE was reached. At 19:30 hours owing to the badly overcrowded roads the Company moved on to PALLIASSE and rested.

Grand Couronné, the worst hill of the lot and from where, on a clear day, Johnny can see as far as Salonika, 50 to 60 miles away. If we can only get that hill and the surrounding ground everything would be O.K. Priority message just came through to move off at 1:00 p.m. Can't stop to write anymore, the guns commenced.

We are now at Palaisse Ravine, so I can write some more. Directly after the message, we got ready, just fighting order[95] and enough signaling kit that was needful in the line.

At 1:00 p.m. up came the lorries, in went our kits and up we all jumped. At 1:30 p.m. full speed up to the line, yelling like a lot of maniacs. At the same time we bluffed Johnny that there were more of us than were really coming by sending more lorries forward than were needed to carry us and our kit. We sped right across the plain and as we knew that Johnny could see us he must have thought there were thousands of us. He tried to stop us with some big 'uns but no damage apart from to the earth. We arrived at Gugunci at 2:00 p.m. but could not go any further as the traffic would not allow it, so we all got out ready to go the rest of the way on foot. There were poor chaps coming down from the line, some with shell-shock, nerves absolutely shattered, equipment half hanging off and clothes torn. It was an awful sight. Can you wonder at it? Three years in this forsaken hole fighting the Bulgar, the Huns, with Turks & Austrians thrown in and the rivers and hills to overcome and not a complaint. I say again, can you wonder at it? All the boys could say as they passed us to a quieter place, with their haggard looks, was: "It's Murder, don't go up there, go back." Only those who have seen it know what it is like. Had a talk with some prisoners: "Ah, Tommy", one said: "We plenty finish" and we thought so too. Then jogged along our way and arrived here at

---

95 Fighting Order is a light scale of equipment carried by a soldier going into action. Generally this would include gas mask, water bottle, entrenching tool and small pack, the latter containing iron rations and additional ammunition that could not be fitted into webbing pouches. Men would often carry a couple of empty sandbags to assist with consolidating ground won. Bombing sections would carry additional grenades and selected platoon would take forward picks and shovels to assist with consolidation of positions.

Paliasse at 7:00 p.m. making it five hours from Gugunci, a distance of a mile and a half. It is 9:30 p.m. so I am going to get a little sleep.

"Up came the lorries, in went our kits and up we all jumped. At 1:30 p.m. full speed up to the line...we bluffed Johnny that there were more of us than were really coming by sending more lorries forward than were needed to carry us and our kit," 18 September 1918

19 September 1918[96]
I had hardly dosed off last night when we had to get up and go up the trenches. Johnny had counterattacked and had driven our boys off the hills. Got into trenches at 1:00 a.m. While on our way and near Castle Hill we had some gas over. On went the helmets and we moved through it, glad it was not mustard. One poor chap forgot to take out his plug and almost choked himself for want of air. It was his own fault, he had never been in the line in all his three years, so I suppose he thought he would never want his helmet. At 5:00 a.m. this morning the boys went over, the 77th Brigade got the Tongue back. My own Brigade, the 66th, were too much cut up, but they got the trenches at Mamelon, Sugarloaf and to the bottom of Grand Couronné inflicting terrible slaughter on the enemy, but could not remain, they were literally blown out of there. From my position D8 on Berk's Hill I saw the good old Jocks go over from Horseshoe Hill. Over they went, but they were driven back. They rallied again and over they went again, but the same thing happened. Then once again they rallied (but all the ranks had dwindled) and they had a third go at 'em with the same result. But what was the matter? I expected to see the French go over who were to help the Jocks. They reached the reserve trench just behind, but did not move.[97] *How Johnny did not see them was on*

---

[96] 66th MGC War Diary, 19 September 1918: "At 0100 on the 19th last 2 sections moved to Oxford camp via PEARSE FOUNTAIN, two to KIDNEY where they remained in Divisional Reserve during the attack on the morning of the 19th. Company Headquarters were in DD8. These sections were not called upon on the evening of the 19th. The Company relieved 4 sections of 65th MGC who remained in the line until the evening of the 20th."

[97] The 2nd Regiment of Zouaves were to have assisted the 9th King's Own (Royal Lancaster) Regiment in the assault on Pip Ridge and to secure the left flank of 77th Brigade. The French troops came under fire as they approached their assembly area, which led their commanding officer to believe they were under Bulgarian observation, despite assurances that this was not the case. He therefore refused to move his troops forward. This failure to advance had serious consequences as the 9th King's Own were left to assault Pip Ridge alone and 77th Brigade had their left flank exposed to enfilade fire. Having no experience of fighting at Doiran the 2nd Zouaves failed to understand the Bulgarian artillery fire plan which laid down barrages on pre-registered

account of the smoke screen we put up in front of his observation post on Grand Couronné or he could have blown them to pieces but all he seemed to think about was his own front lines and ours. The Bulgar was laying the trenches flat, he covered me with earth from one of his big shells. Oh Dear, wind up, but all I got was a cut on the hand. Then shells came fast and furious and seeing a small hole in the side of the trench I lunged my head in (it's remarkable how safe you feel with your head covered up). Our boys pummeled Johnny until 11:00 p.m, let the guns cool and off again at 11:30 p.m. The hill is too much for the boys. The Greeks went over on Petit Couronné and went beyond to another hill, gave Johnny a good hiding, but they were driven back. The Division that I belong to (the 22nd) got cut up so much that we were withdrawn to Pillar Hill and back we crawled in small batches, torn and bleeding, kit just hanging on their shoulders.[98]

20 September 1918
It is the same today, continuous smashing on both sides. They are advancing on the left and right. The Serbs going strong on the left and the French also on Vardar front and our boys on the right, the Strummers Section[99]. *But the Pip Ridge, Hill 535, and Grand Couronné on to Doiran are a bit too much, absolutely impregnable. A fortress of the first order, what a lot of life it has cost the last day or two to try to take them. Streams of wounded coming down all day. At 2:00 p.m. I had to go by myself from Pillar Hill to the old transport lines at Rockley. Got there about 5:00 p.m. carrying fighting order. You can guess how I ended up. As soon as I got there I had to connect up with*

---

positions from where enemy attacks were likely to originate. The French had entered one such zone when they came under fire. The regiment would have escaped the attention of Bulgarian artillery had they pushed on to their assembly area, which had been carefully selected by British staff officers with ample experience of the Doiran battlefield.

[98] Total casualties for the 2nd Battle of Doiran (18-19 September 1918) were 7,103 officers and men, 88% being suffered by XII Corps and the Greek 'Seres' Division in the main attacks against the 9th (Pleven) Division. Total Bulgarian casualties for the battle were 2,726.

[99] A reference to XVI Corps, which had previously served in the Struma Valley.

whoever I could to get messages through to Pillar Hill. There being no infantry lines about, I go to a Small Arms Ammunition Column, got down to it at 9:00 p.m. with the receiver fixed to my ear all night in case anything came through. Slept the sleep of the weary until 8:00 a.m.

21 September 1918[100]
There is still plenty of shelling. I met a French officer today and we had a little talk to pass the time away. He said he had been in France for four years but never experienced such bombardment as here and that is carried unanimously by everyone who has been to France. No messages through except orders for me to remain at old transport lines. Order came in late in day to return to Pillar Hill.

22 September 1918
Went to Three Trees to connect up with D.M.G.O. (Division Machine Gun Officer). Did not have enough wire, went to Vladaja Ravine and got wire. On getting back to Three Trees, was told not to connect with D.M.G.O. but to go up to line again. Johnny is moving off the Pips and Grand Couronné. Oh Glory. Wonders of wonders. The place was ours. The transport came up to Pillar Hill. The first time in three years of fighting the transport has come so near. Johnny now going back at a run. The Serbs and French advancing with all speed on the Vardar. Oh, isn't it joyful? I'd like to hug somebody, even a mule. And dance with him. Johnny is blowing up his dumps and ammunition depots and the blaze is something worth seeing. Well, this is all for today. Our planes are bombing Johnny while on the retreat and sending him a lovely dance.[101] *Oh I'm tired. Goodnight.*

---

100 66th MGC War Diary, 21 September 1918: "The Zouaves took over from No.2, 3, and 4 sections, our machine guns remaining on the line in addition to the French guns."

101 The inability of German and Bulgarian forces to halt the Franco-Serbian advance led to Bulgarian C-in-C General Todorov ordering his 1st Army to pull out of their lines east of the River Vardar during the night of 20 September. Next day RAF aircraft reported columns of Bulgarian troops streaming northward. Whilst moving through the Kresna, Kosturino and

Bulgarian dugouts on the reverse slope of Grand Couronné, 1918.
(IWM HU 89730)

Rupel Passes the Bulgarians were bombed and strafed by the RAF, turning the orderly withdrawal into a rout.

23 September 1918[102]
At 8:30 a.m. we moved off over Horseshoe Hill, when three days ago we dare not show the top of our heads. Through the ruins of Doldzeli Village, past Mamelon and onto the Volovec track, the dead laying everywhere: British, French, Bulgar and German. As we marched through them towards Grand Couronné, a point we thought we would never reach, we stopped at the foot of Grand Couronné at 10:30 a.m. to rest. We went about the Bulgar trenches and dugouts to look for souvenirs. Some of the dugouts went 30 feet into the ground. Charlie and I continued our walk up Grand Couronné. Half way up several explosions occurred and up went some of his dugouts, the Bulgars had laid booby traps. But nobody was harmed, so we went steadily up to the top. We walked on through his barbed wire over to the other side and visited the General Headquarters. What a palace (to what ours were). Tier upon tier of dugouts and shelters, a regular village it was, all out of the way of shells. The best I ever saw, painted and decorated inside like bungalows at Hampton Court. Everything, up to the best of their ability. I bet they hardly knew a war was on! Went to the Observation Post at the top[103] and looked through over our old line. Jove. What a view. (He would never get a better place in a 1000 years). But just below our chaps were laying in pitiful array. War! It's a rotten Game! On the hills below, parties were burying the dead. A Welch Regiment[104] got the furthest up Grand Couronné. What

---

102 66th MGC War Diary, 23 September 1918: "The Company moved with the 66th Infantry Brigade to the MAZE. In the evening they moved to VOLOVEC and camped for the night."
103 The 'Devil's Eye'.
104 The battalion in question was the 7th South Wales Borderers and to honour their part in the battle the unit was awarded the Croix de Guerre by General Franchet d'Esperey. The citation reads:
'A Battalion animated by a remarkable spirit and a lofty sense of duty. On 18th September 1918 under the energetic leadership of Lieutenant Colonel Burges, it attacked the enemy's positions, climbing a steep slope under a hail of shells and the fire of trench mortars and machine guns. In spite of heavy losses it pressed on with no thought but to reach the enemy and thereby gave proof of its tenacity and offensive spirit, and formed an example of self sacrifice worthy of the highest praise.'

DIARY DURING MY PERIOD IN SALONIKA

a struggle it must have been, climbing over rocks, after the Bulgars, while he yelled "Come on Johnny." A Sergeant and Corporal got the furthest only to fall under the fire of Johnny's machine guns. They got to the last belt of wire. We left the observation post and went back to the company with that choking feeling in the throat, thinking and knowing the struggle those boys had gone through. At 5:00 p.m. we moved on to about two miles over the back of Grand Couronné. Each side of the road was littered with nothing but shells and baggage that Johnny had left in his scramble to get away. Timber, horses and mules he unloaded and our aeroplanes bombing him all the way, sweeping down on him and raking his ranks with machine guns, putting him on the run. At 7:00 p.m. we made camp and we go on again in the early morning.

24 September 1918[105]
We went after him again early this morning, over hills, then plain, then hills, fighting all the way. The Bulgar is still retreating. The dumps, he is blowing up miles in front of us, and on 'til dark. The cavalry went into action today, got their chance on a plain but when they reached

---

In addition, Lieutenant Colonel Daniel Burges was awarded the Victoria Cross for his leadership of the battalion that day. His citation reads: 'When still some distance from his objective the battalion came under severe machine-gun fire which caused many casualties among company leaders. Lt.-Col. Burges, though himself wounded, quite regardless of his own safety, kept moving to and fro through his command, encouraging his men and assisting them to maintain formation and direction. Finally, as they neared the enemy's position, he led them forward through a decimating fire until he was hit again twice and fell unconscious. His coolness and personal courage were most marked throughout and afforded a magnificent example to all ranks.'

Burges survived the battle as was taken by the Bulgarians to a dugout behind Grand Couronné, where his wounds were treated. When the 9th (Pleven) Division retreated a few days later, Burges was found by the British.

105 66th MGC War Diary, 24 September 1918: "Moved to the south of HANSALI."

the hills on the other side the Bulgars had some machine guns hidden and well, you can guess the rest![106]

25 September 1918
Went to Volovec village to scrounge round. Went in officer dugout but nothing any good left. We are resting a while before going on. To the right of us is Lake Doiran. Some miles behind you can see the top of Grand Couronné, in front a bit of plain, then the mountain range, Belashitza. The Bulgars are up there, the boys are shelling him with everything. We have received orders to move on for now. I shall pack up. It is 7:00 p.m. and we are near the Bulgar again.

26 September 1918
After sleeping with only one blanket all night in cold, I have a beastly sore throat and cold. The Belashitza range is in our hands and the Bulgars retreated 17 kilos behind during the night. At about 9:00 a.m. across the plain we saw a motorcar carrying a white flag and as it got near, saw it was a staff car with three Bulgarian officers in it. They were being taken to Corps Headquarters. We are under orders to move at any time. Hope we are to go over the Belashitzas as I'd like to see what Bulgaria looks like.

27 September 1918
Parade. Wrote letters with old envelopes as paper. What a struggle to get a bit of paper to write on. Nothing else to do today. Wish they would get a move on and push over the Belashitzas and follow Johnny.

---

[106] Both the Derbyshire and Surrey Yeomanry were in action on 24 September: The Surrey Yeomanry led 65th Brigade onto the Blaga Planina ridge north of Doiran and up along tracks into the Beles Mountains. Here they came under heavy fire and were forced to continue the advance dismounted. By nightfall the regiment's horses were exhausted and without water, which forced the yeomanry to return to camp. The Derbyshire Yeomanry advanced from Furka with 26th Division and the Greek 14th Division. Mounted patrols were sent into Kosturino, Tatarli and Valandovo. As the advance continued the yeomanry came under heavy artillery fire and the main body of the regiment camped that night in cover offered by a valley near Cestovo.

At 10:00 a.m. today Charlie and myself went to a Bulgar camp about 4 kilos away and went in his garden. What a place. After a look round we found a basket, filled it with tomatoes and other kinds of stuff. Got back to camp and showed the boys. Then they all went to the place and raided it, officers as well, or rather their orderlies.

29 September 1918
Mess orderly so could not get out today. One chap, who preferred to remain in camp, I thought would do it for me so that I could make a day of it with Charlie for another scrounge. But being an obliging sort of chap, he refused, so I had to remain in camp. However, I went out in the afternoon and found another garden. Charlie and I carried back as much as we could. I got some fat from the cook and we had fried tomatoes and bully. The fellow who would not take mess orderly expected a share, but was told to go to the Dickens.

September 30, 1918
This morning seemed to be a bit different. Got permission to go out again, went to the Pips, but the old Bulgar camps were awful, the stench turned us sick, so we cleared off. Got back to camp and told to parade. Up marches Lieutenant Eccles with a message in his hands. "Well, Boys'" he says, "I've got good news for you" and he reads out the message – an Armistice has been signed with Bulgaria. Hostilities ceased at 12 p.m. today. Well, that's that! Now let's get out of the damned hole! Wonder where we will go next.

1 October 1918
Everything at a standstill and how quiet everything has been since the cessation of hostilities. It doesn't seem right, one still expects to hear the boom of guns and crack of rifles.

2 October 1918
Went to Pips again and on way back bought canteen stuff.

3 October 1918
Went to the old canteen at Gugunci but it was miles away. Got there eventually and a lorry brought us back. Missed dinner.

4 October 1918
Nothing much doing. Expected to move, washout.

5 October 1918[107]
Prepared to move. I had to report sick and was excused duty. Company moved off. I remained with transport. What a rotten day! Raining all the time. At night we were washed out and fed up.

6 October 1918
Company went to Volovec village. I had to follow with transport. It is still raining. Mud, Mud, Mud, Slip, Slip, Slip. What a happy life, so nice and simple. Went to join company in afternoon. Found my bivvy line and blankets but no bivvy so went and kipped with Charlie.

8 October 1918
Moved to a Bulgar dugout to fix up station. Got in a table and fixed up buzzer.

---

[107] 66th MGC War Diary, 5 October 1918: The Company moved to camp southwest of VOLOVEC and carried out salvage operations. There were signs of heavy fighting on the ORB. Two Greek soldiers were buried, having been found on the wire at the foot of BLACK HILL. Several Bulgars were buried on PITON CHAUVE. Our artillery appeared to have done exceptionally fine counter-battery work. The gun positions, though heavily concentrated, were in many cases severely damaged. The shell holes were rim to rim round nearly all the battery positions. The Bulgar dugouts appeared to be considerably larger and better constructed than our own. There appeared to be no shortage of timber or cement. The principle of defense in dugouts appeared to have been carried out very thoroughly. Dugouts as far back as the face of BLACK HILL appeared to have been actually lived in. Trench mortars were in position at BLACK HILL.

DIARY DURING MY PERIOD IN SALONIKA

9 October 1918
Are to move back near Grand Couronné. Rumor that we are to move on to Turkey and have a cut at them, as the Austrians are finishing. In the afternoon we got to a Bulgar camp and went to one of his dugouts to make that a station. It is very late when we finished so could not run fresh wire to General Headquarters, so we thought we would leave it until morning. Got down to sleep about 10:15 p.m. Then voices shouted "What's that! Get a light someone!" Bugs and other vermin all over us. Why, it's more than we could stick. About 11:30 p.m. we thought laying the wire was better than the bugs and off we went through the rain and bushes until we were wet through. Found another dugout near old camp, lit a fire and got dry and went to sleep.

10 October 1918
Up at 5:00 a.m, finished wiring by 6:30 a.m. and went to canteen. Got milk, biscuits, tinned fruit and had a good supper. When we had another try at going to sleep in the dugout, it was just so bad that I went and slept in the open but that was also bad. The rain drenched us. Went on duty from midnight until 3:00 a.m. One chap's trying to sleep on my table and another in the open trying to do it somehow. Others on the floor of the dugout with their overcoats over them. Are afraid to get between the blankets. Poor bounders, the Bulgars were dirty rotters.

11 October 1918
Moved to Three Trees after a long trek, just about done up

12 October 1918
Still at Three Trees. In the afternoon went to Kirec village, arrived about 9:00 p.m.

13 October 1918
Remained at Kirec.

14 October 1918
Marched to Sarigol via Janes to an old camp.

"While on the march to Lake Langasar, my leg cracked up and the commanding officer gave me his horse to ride," 14 October 1918

15 October 1918[108]
While on the march to Lake Langaza, my leg cracked up and the commanding officer gave me his horse to ride. Had to see doctor and was sent to 68th Field Ambulance.

16 October 1918
Sent to 63rd General Hospital where Doctor saw wound and said that the leg needed rest.

17 October 1918[109]
Went to 8th Convalescent Camp.

---

108 66th MGC War Diary, 15 October 1918: SARIGEUL to DREMIGLAVA.
109 Whilst George went off to hospital and convalescent camp, 66th MGC prepared to head for Dedeagatch as 22nd Division was tasked with initiating the invasion of Turkey from Europe in an attempt to bring about the surrender of the Ottoman Empire. The Company's transport moved off by road on 20 October, whilst the rest of the unit embarked on the destroyer

DIARY DURING MY PERIOD IN SALONIKA

23 November 1918
Discharged from Convalescent Camp and sent to Summer Hill. Arrived about 10:00 a.m. and saw a couple of my pals. Went to canteen for some tea and was told that all fellows from the 66th Brigade were to join company tomorrow and go on to Turkey. But my luck was out, within three hours I was in Hospital again. It happened like this: while returning from canteen at 2:00 p.m. on our way back we had to cross a wide trench. While jumping across it my leg, the wounded one, gave way and sent me to the bottom smashing the other foot. Was in hospital again about 3:00 p.m., leg put in plaster today (the 24th).

19 December 1918
Doctor asked me today if I would like to go to Blighty? Would I like to go to Blighty? If my leg would have let me, I would have jumped out of bed and done a jig! [110]

December 20, 1918
Divisional General Medical Officer visited hospital today and our medical officer picked up my medical chart with all its history on it, showed it to DMGO and said something to him. DMGO put a beautiful

---

HMS Hope on 25 October. When just two hours away from Dedeagatch high winds and rough seas forced the flotilla to return to Stavros. Re-embarking on 27 October, the British force, including 66th MGC, arrived at their destination the following day. An armistice with Turkey came into force at noon on 31 October. On 4 November the British force moved forward to Rumjik and then to Mamamli the next day. By 9 November, the British were back at Dedeagatch and it was here that news reached them of the end of hostilities with Germany on 11 November. The 66th MGC, along with the rest of 22nd Division now began returning to the Stavros area. By 30 November, the Company was in camp at Rendina. During this time the transport section in particular suffered much sickness due to fatigue and the cold weather.

[110] With George preparing to return home, his comrades in 66th MGC remained camped at Rendina throughout December 1918. Most of the men were in good health except for a few cases of diarrhea and bronchitis. But there was no influenza. The animals too picked up condition due to the rest. The unit undertook training for three hours each day and much sport, including boxing, rugby and football was engaged in.

'HS' on the chart: 'Hospital Ship'. So I'm going to Blighty, many envious looks on the faces of the other poor chaps. Am I happy.

"Goodbye Salonika! Hurray for Blighty!" 1 January 1919

DIARY DURING MY PERIOD IN SALONIKA

January 1, 1919[111]

---

[111] 66th MGC War Diary, 1 January 1919: Brigade sports.
2 January 1919: Miners (coal and shale) sent to Base to be demobilized.
6 January 1919: Advanced party of 1 officer and 10 OR sent to JANES to prepare for arrival of Brigade.
7 January 1919: Road party consists of 2 officers and transport proceeding to JANES arriving 12th.
13 January 1919: Main body of company left by rail, arriving new camp on 14th. General: very little machine gun work has been possible during the month owing to education classes, work on demobilization and reconstructing camp. Demobilization: Eighteen NCOs and ORs have been sent to Base for demobilization during the month. Also, four officers.
21 January 1919: Capt. Major E.C. Hudson handed over command of the company to Capt. P.B. Deas and proceeded to Base for demobilization. Health: the health of the company at new camp has been exceptionally good.
1-28 February 1919: Very little training has been done this month owing to rapid demobilization and a great reduction in the numbers of the company. Strength of company as of 1-2-19, 5 officers, 105 ORs. These numbers included 8 ORs detached on courses, etc. Numbers demobilized in classes as under:

	Officers	ORs		Officers	ORs
Miners		7	Forward	4	63
Group u 3	3		In addition on leave	2	3
Over 41		2			
"Q"		5	Time serving	6	
Slipmen		6	Extended service	2	
"A"		19	Totals	6	74
"B"		19			
"C"		2			
"D"		2			
"F"	1	2			
Total	4	63			

The health of the company is exceptionally good.
8 March 1919: Orders received for Coy to move to Base area for disbandment purposes.
9 March 1919: Road party consisting of TPT leave for base area.
11 March 1919: Rail party and guns and equipment leave by rail.
12 March 1919: The company and TPT arrive at VOHANTI in the base area.
25 March 1919: The orders for disbanding of the personnel of the 66th MGC

This morning at about 2:00 a.m. the orderly came rushing round waking everyone up and asking "Are you Hospital Ship?" And those who were and could walk were told to dress and march to the evacuation marquee. Then two orderlies bundled me on to a stretcher and carted me to the marquee also. And to see the boys' faces in smiles was a sight. Everybody was happy.

At 3:00 a.m. we were put in the Red Cross cars and sent to Salonika Harbour and on to Hospital Ship. There goes the throbbing of the screws, we are off. Goodbye Salonika, hurray for Blighty. Why, everybody seems to be blubbering, I feel like it too. Hang it. I suppose we are so damned happy. Anyway, we were off to Blighty and home, so what does it matter. Oh, I'm going to dry up!

FINISH JOHNNY

---

were carried out. The 1914/15 ORs to be demobilized and the 1916 men and all officers to proceed on that day to GBD for reposting.

Epilogue

GEORGE BURFORD RETURNED to England on a hospital ship and spent four months at Alexandra Palace hospital recuperating from his leg injury. He was demobilized on 1 May 1919 after serving four years and 61 days, receiving a pension for the surplus, since he went beyond his four-year enlistment. George met his future wife, Ruth Shelston, around 1920, as evidenced by an entry by him in her autograph book. My mother tells the story that George saw Ruth across a dance hall and told his friend, "that is the girl I will marry." They married in 1924 after a long courtship and emigrated to the United States in 1926. Among his war records at the National Archives in Kew, London, is a letter he wrote in 1925, requesting documentation of his military service:

George and Ruth on a picnic.

Minister of Pensions
Southern Awards Section
Bromyard Avenue
Acton, London W3

12 Evansdale Road
Brixton, SW9

August 9, 1925

Dear Sir,

Owing to the opportunity to emigrate to America, I am writing to ask if you would send me a copy of my army discharge with a letter from someone of standing stating nature of military discharge if any and whether honorably discharged.

This is required by me to place before the American Consul.

Could you please forward this quickly.

Thank you in anticipation.

*Yours faithfully,
G.W. Burford
Late 53385, 66th MG Corp, 22nd Div.*

A letter dated September 22, 1925 to George from the Ministry of Pensions accompanies a copy of his Army Character Certificate and states that only one certificate is required by the American Emigration Authorities.

George worked in Providence, Rhode Island as a French furniture polisher. He owned a home in Johnston, Rhode Island and created a beautiful English garden and tennis court on the property. He assisted the US war effort during the Second World War working with blueprints at the shipyard in Providence as did his wife Ruth, who worked in a munitions factory.

EPILOGUE

George and Ruth during the 1930s.

During that time, his female co-workers wrote down on a chart what they thought of their male co-workers. While most were derogatory, my grandfather was listed: "George Burford – gentleman and scholar." As a gentleman, he never wavered. He took care of his family to his best ability, and, during the Depression, he gave money to his less fortunate neighbors and often allowed strangers to live in a makeshift shelter he created in his garage. George always drove a smart car and dressed well, changing from his suit to his work clothes and back again each day. He was English to the end, and wherever he worked, he insisted upon a break for tea at 4:00 p.m.

Perhaps it was the war that disillusioned him, I cannot say, but he never entered a church, as far as my mother remembers. A Baptist minister came by to talk to him about it, and apparently after a long conversation, a friendship began, the minister visiting my grandfather on Sundays after church, despite George never being convinced to attend Sunday church services. In fact, he had many good friends and loved to entertain. My mother states that he was very funny and could mimic well, leaving his friends and family "in stitches."

George was athletic and would try anything, including skiing in the New England mountains. When the gas was rationed during the war, he rode a Schwinn track bike with wooden-rimmed wheels to work in Pawtucket. He held tennis games in the court he built himself, all players dressed in proper whites. He loved classical music and Edward G. Robinson gangster movies and regularly took my mother on Saturday movies stopping to purchase the latest classical recording, and "fish and chips" on the way home.

Ruth Burford with her daughters Ruth, Judy and the twins Jill and Jean, ca. 1950.

EPILOGUE

George passed away in 1946 at the age of forty-eight after a long struggle with colon cancer. My grandmother was left to raise four daughters alone. She cared for her children in the day and worked the night shift both in a munitions factory throughout the war and later in a garment factory. My mother cared for her sisters from 3:00 p.m. to 11:00 p.m. every day after she got home from school. My grandmother eventually got a day job at the Providence Public Library that she loved. I remember visiting her there and she would bring me the cast-off books, encouraging me to read the classics and giving me the great gift of reading.

Though George Burford marched in the Veteran's Day parade in Rhode Island along with other British veterans, it is unknown if he kept in contact with any of the soldiers from the war. At the time of this writing, I have found the family of George McWilliam who died during in the First Battle of Doiran. I met his great nephew, Stuart Charles, who informed me that the family lost two sons in that war and they were grateful to be given a detailed account of George's death. Along with George McWilliam and Fred Farthing, George Burford's other wartime friend Charlie Muncey survived the war. From surviving documents I have discovered that 53383 Private Charles Howard Muncey was born in 1897 at 34 Hoyl Road, Tooting, London. In 1914 he enlisted in a London Territorial battalion of the Royal Fusilliers. Like George Burford he later transferred to the Machine Gun Corps. His records show that he arrived in Salonika during autumn 1916. At the time of his demob, Charlie held the rank of Lance Corporal.

He married Ada Emma Isabel Rhodes in 1928 and had one son Kenneth in 1929, who sadly died in 1967. Charlie himself died in Wandsworth, London in 1978.

My grandfather died a decade before I was born, so I never had the opportunity to know him. My grandmother, who died when I was ten, affectionately called him "Jock," but I do not recall any stories of the war. Her last words before her death in 1967 were: "Is that you, Jock?"

Since the discovery of his diary and many conversations with my mother, I now realize that he was an extraordinary individual. He survived a horrific war under the most dangerous of circumstances, emigrated to America, bought a home and raised a family until his life was tragically cut short. According to my mother, though he became an American citizen, he missed England and she believes he wanted to return. He only became an American citizen in 1944, when he knew he was seriously ill, in order for his young family to receive social security benefits.

George during the 1940s.

EPILOGUE

A Journey to Macedonia

In May of 2012, I went on a Salonika Campaign Society tour led by Alan Wakefield to FYROM, The Former Yugoslav Republic of Macedonia. Our group consisted of fourteen people, plus the local guides and driver, many had taken the tour before.

I woke up in FYROM on May 2, after a two-day journey from Boston, with stops in London and Thessaloniki (formerly Salonika), Greece. We had crossed the border between Greece and FYROM by bus late the previous night. It was pitch dark, except for the bright lights of the casinos on the border. The bright neon was unexpected, and being exhausted without sleep, I thought for a moment I was in Las Vegas.

We arrived at our hotel in darkness, and it was not until I awoke the next morning that I got my first real look at the countryside. We were on Lake Doiran and the small town that rested aside the lake was not very developed, except for a few modern buildings, much as it might have been a century ago. It was early morning and I was the first one from my group to arrive in the dining room. Other than

View across the Doiran battlefield today with Petit Couronné in the centre and Pip Ridge and Grand Couronné in the background.

me there was a very well behaved team of young athletes in uniform with their couches, probably soccer players. The waiter was an older gentleman who could not speak English, nor could I speak the local language. I told him I was American and he took my face in both hands and said, "American, American." I have never been greeted thus, and was comforted by the unexpected and spontaneously warm welcome, especially after two days of sleepless travel to a former communist country!

During our first day on the battlefields I was struck by the terrain, which is rugged, beautiful and remarkably peaceful. Viewing the lush green vegetation that now covers the area one has a hard time imagining the thunder of artillery and the bloodshed of war. One of our guides, Binko, showed us the many herbs that grow in the hills and one could not help but be impressed and comforted by the healing power of nature. The yellow blossoms of Spanish broom covered the mountains and the scent is intoxicating. The contrast with the images of the war from century-old photographs is stark.

The second thing that astounded me was the large expanse of land that my grandfather had to traverse. The size of the mountains, hills and ravines are much larger than I expected and the distances between locations he describes in the diary are much further. His tasks of range finding, firing, and signals were complicated by the diverse terrain which is a contrast to the flat fields of France and Belgium for which he had been trained. I was easily disoriented as we hiked to different locations, and it was difficult to identify where the lines of battle were drawn, as there were so many hills, mountains, ravines and valleys. As we reached each destination, an entirely different perspective revealed itself. I thought about how well my grandfather must have known every perspective with his task as rangefinder and machine gunner.

Throughout the tour, I wished my grandfather was with me, especially when we came across the ruins of bunkers and trenches among familiarly named locations. I must say, I felt a tap upon my shoulder on a number of occasions that seemed to parallel my grandfather's experience, reminders of some of his experiences from the diary. For example, we got lost while trying to hike down from Grand Couronné. While our experience was comical as we hacked through a century's worth of undergrowth, I thought about my grandfather's arrival and getting lost on the way to the trenches. "Damned, we are lost!" On another occasion, our group found a snake along the road, and I was reminded of when my grandfather flung the snake in the air causing his pals to run in different directions.

Doiran British Cemetery with the Memorial to the Missing on the hilltop behind.

One memory that will always stay with me was when a few of us, who were first timers and had never visited the British Memorial to the Missing, headed back over the Greek border to see the memorial as the sun was setting. We had to rush to be back with the group before dark, so we hiked very quickly up the hill to where this impressive and lonely structure stands above the Doiran battlefields at a point close to the center line occupied by the Allied forces. It is a grand and beautiful memorial with the names of more than 2,000 of the fallen who have no known grave so their names are engraved upon the large towering walls. Two large sculpted lions adorn the top one looking peacefully into Greece where the British lines used to be, whilst the other snarles towards the hills beyond Doiran once held by the Bulgarian Army. As we walked around the memorial, the full moon appeared and it reminded me of when my grandfather was at sentry duty looking up at the moon when snipers took shots at him.

Traveling with members of the Salonika Campaign Society was a gift. They were aware of the emotional aspects of my journey and I will never forget their kindness, interest, generosity and helpfulness. I carried my grandfather's diary with me and we read portions throughout the tour. One particular moment was especially moving, when Alan Wakefield read a portion after a long hike up to the Devil's Eye. This is the spot where my grandfather viewed the carnage of the Second Battle of Doiran and for the first time openly questions the war with the simple statement: "war: it's a rotten game!"

The members of the Salonika Campaign Society not only collectively hold a vast knowledge of the war that is invaluable to our understanding of history, they are also "keepers of the flame," honouring the fallen and their efforts to preserve the battlefields and cemeteries. At each cemetery, we read names of the fallen and stopped to say a prayer:

> "They shall grow not old, as we that are left grow old; Age shall not weary them nor the years condemn. At the going down of the sun and in the morning, We will remember them."

EPILOGUE

The 10th (Irish) Division Memorial near Rabrovo in FYROM.

As well as mine, there were other specific interests among the group. Two fellow travelers from Ireland led us to the 10th (Irish) Division Memorial. There, Sean Connolly told us of Irish units and their struggle against appalling weather conditions and the onslaught of the Bulgarian Army during the winter of 1915 and Seamus Greene sang a very stirring rendition of "Danny Boy."

The BE 12 aircraft in which Lieutenant Paul Denys Montague was shot down and killed on 29 October 1917.

Another location visited was the site where Lieutenant Paul Denys Montague of the Royal Flying Corps fatally crashed on 29 October 1917. The crash site had been recently identified by SCS members using archive photographs held at the Imperial War Museum, combined with Google Earth and old fashioned legwork on the ground. Paul Montague, educated at Bedales School and Caius College, Cambridge, was a gifted young naturalist and musician who could even turn his hand to the making of his instrument of choice, the lute. Although a good pilot, Montague stood little chance when he was attacked by a number of German aircraft whilst escorting bombers raiding an ammunition dump. Shot down behind Bulgarian lines, Montague was listed as Missing in Action until a photograph of his body lying beside his aircraft was dropped over a British airfield by the Germans asking for the identity of the pilot as they wished to record his name on the stone they had raised over his grave. Despite the British supplying details, in the post-war chaos of the Balkans the location of the grave was lost and Paul Denys Montague is now commemorated on the British Salonika Force Memorial to the Missing overlooking Lake Doiran. Although his grave will probably never be found, it was fitting to remember this talented individual at the place he fell to earth. His story stands for so many of those lost during the First World War.

As we hiked the many mountains and ravines, the amount of shrapnel, shells and other remnants of war unearthed the past and the realization of how much this part of the world has suffered. Despite the suffering, my heart was lifted by my experiences with the wonderful people of the new nation of FYROM, whose lives go on amidst the ruins of so many past civilizations and wars. The people of the Balkans have had more than their fair share of destruction, and I wish them peace.

Another highlight of the tour was visiting a Turkish Festival in the tiny village of Calikli. Despite the remoteness of the village, it was an international event with groups from all over the Balkans and beyond. Among the many officials in attendance was the President of Macedonia. The goodwill was palpable as each speech called for cooperation and understanding. Experiencing the wonderful

EPILOGUE

music, costumes and the young people, so proud of their culture, is a tribute to the people of this land and their survival despite century deep conflicts.

Hiking along the trails of the battlefield, my companions and I would often break into song. Many knew the songs of Great War, and taught me a few verses. On that note, I will conclude with the song my grandfather sang when he "went mad" after the deaths of his pals Georgie McWilliam and Fred Farthing in the first Battle of Doiran – 'Take me back to dear old Blighty':

> Jack Dunn, son of a gun, over in France today,
> Keeps fit doing his bit up to his eyes in clay.
> Each night after a fight to pass the time along,
> He's got a little gramophone that plays this song:
>
> Take me back to dear old Blighty!
> Put me on the train for London town!
> Take me over there,
> Drop me ANYWHERE,
>
> Liverpool, Leeds, or Birmingham, well, I don't care!
> I should love to see my best girl,
> Cuddling up again we soon should be,
> WHOA!!!
>
> Tiddley iddley ighty,
> Hurry me home to Blighty,
> Blighty is the place for me!
> Bill Spry, started to fly, up in an aeroplane,
>
> In France, taking a chance, wish'd he was down again.
> Poor Bill, feeling so ill, yell'd out to Pilot Brown:
> "Steady a bit, yer fool! we're turning upside down!"
>
> Take me back to dear old Blighty!
> Put me on the train for London town!

TAKE ME BACK TO BLIGHTY

Take me over there,
Drop me ANYWHERE,
Liverpool, Leeds, or Birmingham, well, I don't care!

I should love to see my best girl,
Cuddling up again we soon should be,
WHOA!!!

Tiddley iddley ighty,
Hurry me home to Blighty,
Blighty is the place for me!

Jack Lee, having his tea, says to his pal MacFayne,
"Look, chum, apple and plum! it's apple and plum again!
Same stuff, isn't it rough? fed up with it I am!
Oh! for a pot of Aunt Eliza's raspb'ry jam!"

Take me back to dear old Blighty!

Put me on the train for London town!
Take me over there,
Drop me ANYWHERE,
Liverpool, Leeds, or Birmingham, well, I don't care!

I should love to see my best girl,
Cuddling up again we soon should be,
WHOA!!!

Tiddley iddley ighty,
Hurry me home to Blighty,
Blighty is the place for me!

EPILOGUE

The restored 22nd Division Memorial behind Grand Couronné at Doiran.